# SOCIOLOGY
## AND THE FIELD OF
# EDUCATION

17162

*Prepared for the*
*American Sociological Society*

*By* ORVILLE G. BRIM, JR.

Sociologist, Russell Sage Foundation

LC189
.B855

# RUSSELL SAGE FOUNDATION
New York                                           1958

© 1958

RUSSELL SAGE FOUNDATION

Printed in the United States
of America

*Library of Congress
Catalog Card Number: 58-13045*

WM. F. FELL CO., PRINTERS
PHILADELPHIA, PA.

# CONTENTS

# FOREWORD

THERE IS AN INSISTENT NEED to find ways of channeling the work of the investigator into the hands of those who are the practitioners working on the day-by-day problems of a going society—the administrator, the physician, the judge and correctional officer, the schoolteacher, the social worker, the clergy, and others. To meet that need is the main objective of this series of studies published by Russell Sage Foundation for the American Sociological Society. The wide and sustained response to preceding publications in this series is one measure of their usefulness and of the value of this endeavor.

The increasing interest among sociologists in research on education during the past decade, the current painstaking appraisal of American educational policies and procedures by educators and the general public, and the greater understanding that interpersonal relations, cultural values, conceptions of one's self, and many other matters lying in the realm of sociology are fundamental aspects of the educational process, combine to make the appearance of this bulletin a timely one.

*Sociology and the Field of Education* is the third study published in this series, each one of which focuses upon one major area of practice. In this study Dr. Brim concentrates upon the field of education in the United States. He brings to the task a breadth of interest and rich experience extending back into his own family's distinguished educational leadership. His analysis of each chapter topic proceeds through three stages of attention. There is first a stock-taking of the work done, then an appraisal of accumulated resources, and finally a projection into developmental planning. These are large assignments and the available space is limited. Dr. Brim deals with the material in a mood of systematic

5

probing and makes no claim of finality in his evaluations. He stresses throughout the dual contributions of sociological research in education both to general sociology and to educational practice. His aim is to sharpen the sociological focus on educational processes, and to provoke further work.

The advisory committee for this bulletin consisted of Dr. Wilbur Brookover of Michigan State University, Dr. W. W. Charters of Washington University, Dr. Stephen M. Corey of Teachers College, Columbia University, Dr. Nelson N. Foote of General Electric Company, Dr. Neal Gross of Harvard University, and Dr. Wilbert E. Moore of Princeton University. The general editorial committee for the series consists of Dr. Leonard S. Cottrell, Jr., representing Russell Sage Foundation, and Dr. Wellman J. Warner, representing the American Sociological Society.

The first two bulletins in this series were *Sociology and the Field of Corrections* by Lloyd E. Ohlin, and *Sociology and the Field of Mental Health* by John A. Clausen. In preparation for publication in the near future are three additional studies: *Sociology and the Field of Medical Practice* by Albert F. Wessen of the University of Vermont; *Sociology and the Field of Military Management* by Morris Janowitz of the University of Michigan; *Sociology and the Field of Social Work* by Henry J. Meyer, Jr., of the University of Michigan.

June 1, 1958                                   WELLMAN J. WARNER
                                *Secretary, American Sociological Society*

# I

# INTRODUCTION

THE PURPOSE OF THIS BULLETIN is twofold. The major part attempts a review of basic research studies of the institution of education which have employed the concepts and theories of sociology; it seeks also to indicate those areas of study which have been neglected by sociologists. The last chapter considers the occupational roles which the sociologist has taken, and potentially could take, so as to further his contributions to education through theory and research.

In the review which follows the effort is made to show how sociological research on education can contribute both to the growth of general sociological theory and to the solution of practical operating problems of the educational institution. For the sociologist, the formal educational system of this country constitutes what is probably his richest and most accessible natural source of raw data on personality and social interaction; it needs only to be systematically mined by careful research. For the educator, the important issues he faces in his daily work center almost without exception on interpersonal relations—between teachers, between pupils, between teacher and pupil, between faculty and community—and the continuing attention of the sociologist to such issues cannot fail to illuminate and sharpen one's understanding of these specific social processes.

For example, a study of the differential treatment of students by teachers according to the social class of the former is seen both as a partial explanation of the dropout of lower-class children from school, and as a substantive contribution to the theory of stratification. A study of the relations of school superintendents to their school boards appears both as a fundamental contribution to our understanding of school administration and as an impor-

7

tant contribution to the theory of role conflict. Research on the teacher's handling of the recalcitrant child in the classroom helps the educator in maintaining necessary order and also further develops the sociologists' understanding of the general process of deviance and social control. In sum, we stress throughout this review the dual functions of sociological research on education: its contributions both to sociological theory and to educational practice.

This review is limited to research on elementary, secondary, and higher educational systems. Considerations of space in a bulletin already overly long have prevented our dealing with two important segments of education. The first is graduate training. The very wealth of materials here, informal and otherwise, on training in the various professions has prohibited their inclusion because they could not receive the attention due them. Fortunately, research and writing by sociologists on the professions is a rapidly growing enterprise, and these materials are gradually being integrated within a systematic sociological framework.

The second omission is that of the many informal educational processes which pervade American society, such as educational television and other mass media; nor have we included the vast and expanding field of adult education occurring in churches, unions, business firms, and elsewhere. Absence of their consideration here should not lead one into the error of minimizing their importance. In research on these educational activities, as with those of the formal school systems, the contributions of the sociologist would be of primary importance.

## Historical Background

During any regular school day about one-fifth of the population, or 35,000,000 children and adults in American society, are directly involved in formal school and college activities. Almost every person spends a major portion of twelve years of his life within the formative environment of the educational institution, and a constantly increasing number devotes some sixteen years to formal educational training. These critical facts have commanded the attention of sociologists, although with varying emphasis and enthusiasm, through the past half-century.

Although analysts of the social scene from Plato on have dealt with the institution of education, and eminent sociologists of the last century, such as Spencer and Ward, discussed education, these early works are usually prescriptive and speculative in nature and not research studies. The first work to present a systematic institutional treatment of education was John Dewey's *School and Society*. The following fifteen years saw the publication of some half-dozen books with the same point of view. In 1916 Dewey's *Democracy and Education* stimulated even greater interest in the area, and in the two decades which followed the field gained wide recognition in sociology. During this period numerous colleges began offering courses in sociology and education; the National Society for the Study of Educational Sociology was organized; the *Journal of Educational Sociology* was initiated; and approximately twenty-five texts or major treatises on sociology and education were published.

For the subsequent ten or fifteen years up until the recent past, one surmises that sociological interest in education failed to keep pace in its expansion with the main body of sociology. While no comparative data are available for different time periods, it is clear that the study of education was not a major concern of sociology during this time. An examination of eight leading introductory texts in sociology published just prior to 1950, shows four of them providing no treatment of education; in two, education is not indexed as a subject. In an analysis of publications for the decade 1940–1950, Conrad (A-2) reports that only 2.3 per cent of the articles in the *American Sociological Review* fall into the area of sociology and education.

Certain reasons may be advanced to account for what seems to have been a lagging interest, even though they cannot constitute a full explanation. First, we have noted that earlier writings were programmatic and polemic rather than scientific. With certain notable exceptions, these characteristics continued in sociological writings on education during the time when the main body of sociology was struggling to free itself from the cast of moral philosophy.

Second, and again with some outstanding exceptions, those sociological works on education which were of a research nature used comparatively primitive research techniques. Conrad's review shows that, of the studies appearing during the decade 1940–1950, only a fraction used standard tests, interviews, or observation, and almost no study was reported which used experimental techniques. This was occurring while the main body of sociology was moving strongly in the new direction of increased refinement and rigor in research.

Third, the greater share of research on education had been concerned with limited operating problems, and little effort was made to formulate these problems in the theoretical terms of sociology so that their study advanced both sociology and the practice of education. Important successes in this venture have been made recently, but their relative absence in earlier years served to portray the study of education as a dull process from which the sociologist himself benefited very little.

The result of the three facts mentioned so far is that of the thousand or more articles or books from the past twenty-five years which fall in this area, perhaps less than 10 per cent can legitimately be classed as sound research studies, carried on within a well-defined sociological frame of reference.

A fourth reason which may be advanced to account for this lack of interest on the part of the sociologist is that much the larger part of research on education has been carried on by persons trained in disciplines other than sociology. The consequent impression in many quarters was that the important research areas in education had been preempted by other disciplines, especially psychology. This clearly is not the case—indeed, many of the important research areas have been neglected—but the impression doubtless turned away many sociologists from serious pursuits in the educational field.

For these reasons, among others, sociologists during the past several decades have not been attracted to the study of education in numbers proportionate to the importance of the institutional field, and sociology has yet to make the many contributions which its resources make possible.

An impressive change in the general situation has occurred since about 1950. It is accurate to say that there has been a rapid growth of interest in studies of the educational institution; and in recent years a greater number of both well-established and younger sociologists competent to carry on research programs of good quality have moved into this area. Standards of research have risen, and recognized areas of sociological theory pertaining to social class, small groups, roles, and occupational mobility, to name but a few, are being brought to bear on the several aspects of the educational system.

The change is indicated not only by the growth of research, as will be evident throughout the pages which follow, but by the appearance of systematic appraisals of the field. Recently three general texts of excellent quality (A-1, A-3, A-5) have appeared which summarize much of the sociological literature in the area. In addition, a well-selected collection of the outstanding research articles of recent years is available (A-6). A stimulating appraisal of possible areas of research in education is currently in press (A-4), and delineates a series of problems of direct relevance to sociological theory.

The general expansion of sociology in this country since World War II, and the fact that the many sociologists trained in the postwar period seek new fields in which to do research, are certainly contributing causes of this change. Of perhaps greater importance is the increase in government and foundation funds available for support of research on education. This reflects, in turn, the current societywide interest in its educational system. For example, the Carnegie Corporation of New York, the Fund for the Advancement of Education, the Kellogg Foundation, and Russell Sage Foundation conduct significant programs in education, and the Office of Education of the federal government now supports research in education through its recently established cooperative research program.

## A Classification of Materials in Sociology and Education

It has been our aim to review about one hundred basic references which constitute a fundamental bibliography in the field. We have selected first by merit, and secondly in terms of coverage of topics, both in data and bibliography. This means that the publications cited carry with few exceptions an excellent bibliography in the area with which they are concerned. Where merit and coverage were equal, we chose in terms of recency and, finally, in terms of accessibility.

There are several ways in which one might classify the research in this field. One is to use the traditional topics in education, such as curriculum, method, and teacher training, as a basis. In such a classification, however, the sociological aspect often gets lost, and it is difficult to relate these concepts to the main areas of sociological theory. Another type of classification would emphasize the traditional sociological subdivisions and ask, for example, what contributions have been made by research in education on social stratification, small groups, or community organization. This approach has been taken in recent publications (A-1, A-4). It seems, however, to limit the areas of research in education to the current interests of sociology, rather than letting the characteristics of the educational process raise new theoretical problems for sociology and thus lead it to greater development.

In this bulletin we have sought a scheme which organizes the studies in a logical way, and yet which constitutes a fairly loose and flexible system of classification easily grasped, commonly used, and adaptable to many special interests. We have chosen to use a simple institutional analysis drawing primarily on the concepts of Malinowski.[1] We hold no special brief for this approach; it simply has appeared, after much consideration, to be at this stage of development of the sociology of education the approach which most successfully bridges the gap between the traditional educational problems and the main stream of sociological development.

The five major problems in institutional analysis might be described as follows. First, an institutionalized activity such as education is designed to achieve certain ends for its members and/or for society at large or its subgroups, and hence is regulated toward the pursuit of institutionalized aims. Second, material resources (money or other goods) must be allocated to the

---

[1] Malinowski, Bronislaw, *A Scientific Theory of Culture and Other Essays.* University of North Carolina Press, Chapel Hill, 1944.

institution as a whole from those available to society, and subsequently must be allocated within the institution. Third, personnel must be recruited into the institution to carry out the activities necessary to achieve the aims. Hence, the recruitment, selection, training, and allocation of such personnel to different positions in the institution must be accomplished, these tasks customarily being guided by the aims of the institution. Fourth, the appropriate attitudes and behavior for the members of the institution must be specified, and the performance of these roles assured. The prescribed roles are always based on implicit or explicit ideas held by institutional members and/or by society at large as to how members should behave in order best to realize the aims of the institution. Finally, the institutional activity has results in fact, both for members and for society, which may or may not be recognized and which may or may not be consonant with the avowed aims. Both the intended and unintended functions of the institution require consideration. These points yield the five analytic categories of aims, allocation of materials, allocation of personnel, roles, and functions.

The research on these institutional components is of many types. There are descriptive studies of single components, such as Terrien's report (F-29) on role prescriptions for teachers in an elementary school system. There are descriptive studies of another kind, which though concerned with a single institutional element provide comparative data either between different educational organizations, such as Holland's research (E-9) on student recruitment into two different types of colleges, or between educational and other institutions, such as the Ruml and Tickton report (C-5) on educational salaries in contrast to those of other groups.

There are analytical studies relating one institutional component to another. The work can deal with a single school or college, as in Gordon's intensive study (G-11) of a single high school. The research may involve comparative study of several educational systems, as in the current research by Neal Gross and his colleagues at Harvard, dealing with the relation between consensus on institutional aims and the functioning of institutions, and in the work by James Coleman at the University of Chicago which compares the effects of student peer group culture upon academic performance in two high schools.

Finally, there are analytic studies relating characteristics of the educational system to other systems of the society; that is, they are studies of the effect of another institutional area, such as religion, upon the educational institution. As above, these may be done either on a single case basis as in Hollingshead's work (F-18) on the effects of social class on student roles in one school, or on a comparative basis, such as Mulhern's treatment (B-13) of cultural influence on the aims of education in different historical periods.

Our subsequent review indicates clearly that most research falls into the first class, providing descriptive data on various elements of the educational system. The analytic studies are mostly of single educational systems, constituting, as it were, case studies of the relation between elements within an educational system or between an educational system and some other institution. While such studies constitute a solid basis for further advances, part of the overall strategy for sociology in the field of education must be to undertake more analytic studies on broad samples of educational systems.

# II

# THE AIMS OF EDUCATION

WITH RESPECT to the first institutional component, that of educational aims, sociology has given its weakest performance. Our overview here may seem abbreviated, but its shortness comes instead from the fact that there have been very few research efforts directed to appraising educational aims, or their relation to other institutional components.

## Educational Aims and Cultural Values

The most important tradition in the sociological analysis of the aims of education has been the study of the relation between such aims and the general values of society, with special reference to the social control over the aims of education. The primary conclusion supported by this research is that the aims of education are in the last analysis prescribed and legitimized by the community (or society) in which the institution exists. When the culture becomes so complex that it cannot be transmitted without an additional formal system, a separate educational structure arises. This institutional enterprise is chartered by society to train society's members for adequate adult role performance. The aims of education are consonant with the conceptions of the ideal adult which society wishes to produce, and the educational institution possesses legitimate power to pursue its aims only to the extent that they are in fact those which society considers desirable.

This conclusion has been documented in many ways. It was Durkheim's major contribution in his work on education (B-3) to analyze this problem, deducing that the aims of education vary according to different types of societies. Cross-cultural data indicative of this conclusion are presented in two publications (B-8, B-19), while culture-historical analysis has resulted in two important works which attest to shifts in educational aims in accord with shifts in a society's ideals for the kind of person held desirable (B-1, B-13).

This research does not lead one, however, to a necessary conclusion that the aims of education are always conservative, in the sense that they are only to conserve and transmit the existing culture to a new generation. Several examples will come to mind. Thus, where society values the pursuit of invention and discovery with its consequent changes, it sanctions such aims in its institutions. One legitimized purpose of higher education is to produce members of society trained to play the role of innovator. Where society has undergone continual changes, and is oriented toward further (and unforeseen) changes in the future, it may charter its schools to prepare its children for such change by developing critical attitudes toward their current culture and through improving their creative and judgmental skills, so that as adults they can more readily lay aside obsolete cultural patterns and produce new ones appropriate to the times. Last, from a parent's point of view he may wish and prescribe for the schools that they not limit themselves to simply teaching the child the culture which the parent has, but rather that they enrich the child beyond the cultural resources of the local community, so that the child excels the parent in both wisdom and achievement in the world.

In the foregoing instances one must still recognize that the nonconservative aims of education derive their legitimacy from the fact that society sanctions the pursuit of new, nontraditional goals. This leads to a second problem in the study of the relation of educational aims to broader cultural values, namely, the degree to which change or variation in such aims can be accomplished without the support of the larger society.

The studies cited suggest that it is a mistaken notion to treat the educational system as a means whereby a social revolution is effected through production of a new generation of adults seeking new values. This point needs stressing because there are many who continue to think otherwise, and who fail to see that in fact the educational system of a society is the means whereby traditional culture is preserved, and that any new values it transmits

within one generation are fractional compared to the massive
tradition it imparts. In American education, for instance, this
erroneous viewpoint reached its extreme in the 1930's when there
was a strong demand that the school educate for a new social
order.

How, then, do protagonists of new educational aims influence
the area of education? The sociologist will recognize this as the
problem of the "great man" in cultural change, and it would
seem that comments on the general problem are applicable here.
Thus, on the one hand, one argues that any solitary influence
upon educational aims reflects the fact that the larger society is
changing, and the individual has successfully anticipated and led
such change. On the other hand is the fact that individuals do
introduce new values into their society which are taken up if the
time is right, or which in any case help to move public opinion
toward the acceptance of the new value at a later time.

The research relating educational aims and cultural values has
shown the dependence of the former on the latter. What has not
been dealt with are the more critical problems mentioned above.
With respect to the question of conservatism in educational aims,
one could with profit study the social conditions under which
aims of education emerge which demand educating for inde-
pendence and creativity, and where the ideal image of the adult
is a person unburdened by the tradition of the past. Enough
natural variation in communities and societies exists so that the
social scientist need not wait upon historical change to grapple
with this problem.

A start has been made in a research program at the University
of Wisconsin which involves comparisons between communities.
One report (B-11) on a large number of communities matched
except for homogeneity and heterogeneity in ethnic and religious
characteristics shows heterogeneous communities to be more
favorable to breaking with traditional aims, a finding congruent
with anthropological research on culture contact and culture
change.

With respect to the question of achieving change in educational
aims, one could inquire into the role of the private school in

American society. Under a democratic system, the public school seeks the ends of the majority, but the innovator at odds with society is free to build his own educational system. Most private schools are to be understood as systems which are chartered by, and derive their power from, dissident subgroups of the society who hold their own conception of the valuable adult.

If it is true that the values represented in such schools are sometimes adapted, and sometimes not, into the public system, why is this true? If such schools are viewed as experimental laboratories of culture change, by what means do their results become known to society, so that their influence upon the educational system is actually achieved?

### What Aims Do People Hold for the Educational System?

The general consideration introduced above, that aims held for education reflect one's conception of the desirable adult in society, leads to the conclusion that one will find different aims where there are different values. A major neglected area of research has been the simple description of differences in aims for education, and the relation of these to one's age, occupation, religion, and other socioeconomic variables. For example, Dahlke (A-3) has delineated five value orientations and conceptions of the good man which underlie differences in the aims of educational systems: the religious, the nativist, the market, the common man, and the humanist orientations. However, the author cannot show with any concreteness, because of the lack of data, the way in which the value orientations are manifested in specific educational aims, and the effort is primarily illustrative of the approach one might take in relating general values to institutional aims.

With respect to the aims of educators, there are a great number of individual statements to be found in educational writings, but these most often are isolated expressions of personal opinion. In contrast, several important efforts have been made to prepare a statement of aims which is agreed upon by representative groups of educators. Such statements of aims are incorporated in the code of ethics of the National Education Association, in the report of the President's Commission (B-15), and in a widely accepted statement of objectives by the Educational Policies Commission (B-4). Recently two volumes pertaining to the objectives of elementary and secondary schools have appeared (B-5, B-9). The latter describe objectives in behavioral rather than subject-matter learning terms, and express the beliefs of a select committee of educators.

Such statements should provide a suggestive range of problems from which sociologists could develop more specific and manageable questions for research. A major effort in this direction has been made by Neal Gross and his colleagues in the Harvard Graduate School of Education. A forthcoming book (B-6) reports on the beliefs of school superintendents, and later publications will describe the aims of education held by a sample of New England teachers.

Also needed is systematic information regarding the public's aims for education. Fragments of survey data pertaining to these aims tend to be scattered widely through various publications. Martin Trow of the University of California at Berkeley currently is preparing a compilation and analysis of these survey findings which will make them more easily accessible to the sociologist.

At present only a few major studies have dealt directly with public aims for education. A national opinion survey (B-17) of several years ago of what is most important in education shows variation by the education of the respondent: an emphasis on character education is positively correlated with educational status, while a concern for the usual subject matter, e.g., arithmetic, shows an inverse relation. Age comparisons show younger respondents (twenty-one to thirty-nine years) to stress social adjustment much more than do persons forty or older, suggesting the validity of recent arguments that our conception of the desirable man may be changing toward one whose primary virtue is to get along with others.

With respect to the much studied "school board," a number of studies over the past years have described the socioeconomic background of board members, with the implication that the aims of the institution will reflect class interests of such members.

Charters (B-2) has pointed out, however, that research on the actual aims of school board members, or on whether school aims differ with the differing composition of school boards, has not as yet been done. The forthcoming work by Gross and others mentioned above will report data on the correlates of attitudes of educational progressivism among a sample of New England school board members, so that the situation Charters describes will be in part rectified.

With respect to aims held by students in different types of schools, a major source of data regarding the aims of higher education is contained in a forthcoming work from Cornell on the values of American college students. This study uses a sample of over 4,500 students at ten different universities. Preliminary results (B-20) show over two out of three students state the major purpose of higher education to be that of providing a basic general education, or vocational and professional training. Smaller percentages mentioned learning to get along with others. Essentially the same finding occurs in a large sample survey by Slocum (B-18) of secondary school students planning for college, and in national opinion surveys (B-14, B-17) which include questions on aims in sending sons and daughters to college. The latter two surveys, it should be added, are repositories of a variety of information on public attitudes toward education.

These results may seem to state the obvious, but they gain importance when contrasted with national survey data on high school students regarding the aims of the high school. The Purdue Public Opinion Poll (B-16) reports the three major student responses to the question of what people should get out of high school: 36 per cent of the students rate first knowing how to get along with other people; 33 per cent stress a sense of discipline and responsibility; and only 17 per cent emphasize basic subjects like English, or knowledge about our society. The findings thus indicate a radical difference in the aims of students in secondary and higher educational institutions, or, perhaps, in the goals of older and younger citizens as noted earlier; in either event it spurs one to ask why, as well as what other, value differences may obtain?

While the descriptive study of the objectives of education held by different groups may seem of little import, there are at least two ways in which such information would be of value. First, the descriptive data are a necessary foundation for research on the relation of aims to other aspects of the culture, as suggested above, and for research on intra-institutional relations, as indicated below. Second, by virtue of the fact that educational aims reflect one's values, express his fundamental beliefs regarding the desirable attributes of man, such descriptive data provide an insight into the basic values held by society's members. It is an extremely sad commentary on current social science that we know almost nothing of the aspirations of man for the kind of person he wants to become, and wants his children to become. Even the literature on socialization where one would expect to find these facts has emphasized the description of parent behavior and presents fewer than a half-dozen studies of the characteristics parents desire for their children. The study of aims sought through education by various groups would in addition to its contributions to educational practice itself help to fill this gap in our knowledge.

### The Relation of Aims to Other Institutional Components

An almost completely neglected area of research seems to be that of the influence of educational aims upon other aspects of the educational structure, and, indeed, the reverse process whereby aims are altered to be congruent with the realities of the educational situation. We have mentioned already the work to be reported by Gross and his colleagues on the relation of aims to the satisfaction of institutional personnel. The few other studies which bear on this problem (e.g., G-11) describe the way in which aims of an educational system influence the role prescriptions and performance of members of the system, and are discussed in connection with the latter topic.

The fact is, therefore, that there are many problems awaiting attention in this area. For example, a systematic description of the aims of education would undoubtedly reveal that many of them conflict with each other, and hence some are not truly achievable. The question arises of how educational personnel resolve this conflict in allocating their efforts to achievement of one or another aim, and of how such conflict influences morale and career satisfaction.

Another among the many questions of importance in this area is the way in which educational systems solve the problem of disparity of aims held by their personnel. Is it true that educational personnel are recruited, and probably promoted, in schools and colleges to the extent that their goals for education are the same as those of their superiors who control hiring and advancement? And what of the students? There can be little doubt that for many students what they hope to get out of school is markedly different from what their teachers hope the student will get; indeed, it is very clear that for many students their desires actually conflict with those of their instructors. Unlike other institutions, education cannot isolate or exclude from its personnel except under extreme conditions those groups who do not share the dominant goals of the institution. Education has the inescapable problem of somehow integrating the various aims of its two major bodies of personnel, the educators and students. If the enduring solution is that the student gradually changes and accepts the beliefs of his teachers with respect to the value of education, how is this actually accomplished?

As a final instance, consider the relation between a preferential ranking of aims and the degree to which their achievement can be objectively measured. It has been pointed out that many of the stated aims of education are general in nature, and in their present form their achievement is not scientifically measurable. What are the effects upon an institution of pursuing ends when it cannot know if, or when, it achieves them? How does one evaluate the effectiveness of different means in this situation? How is the performance of personnel to be evaluated? Is it true, as we suggest later, that general, unappraisable ends serve the function of protecting educators (and, in other contexts, other professional groups) from public control since the public has no way of determining if a good job is being done? On the other hand, it is true that certain functions of education are measurable (e.g., the performance of New York secondary school students on the Regents' examination). It is true also that that which is measurable becomes used as the criterion of success when one is evaluating procedures and personnel, so that the institution becomes increasingly oriented toward achievement of measurable outcomes, to the detriment of the more general, and usually more highly desired, goals. To put the question generally, then: how do educational systems solve the dilemma posed by pursuing general and unmeasurable ends while at the same time having the need to evaluate the effectiveness of their own institutional procedures?

None of these problems would seem to be limited to education alone. While their study would have direct implications for educational systems, both the theory and data produced would necessarily contribute to the general comparative analysis of social structure.

# III

# THE ALLOCATION OF MATERIALS

THE ALLOCATION of materials to institutions within a society must provide for two basic things. It must be sufficient to motivate the necessary personnel to enter the institution and to continue an adequate performance of duties, and it must provide the means necessary for the achievement of its aims. At first glance the problems of distribution of wealth by a society among its component institutions may strike one as a topic belonging to economics. Even brief reflection, however, makes it clear that the allocation process is regulated by social values and the distribution of power in society, and that the contributions of sociological study of this process would be significant.

## The Support of Education as a Whole

It is a basic social fact that the institutions of society compete with each other for materials and for personnel, that these are always in short supply, given the ultimate aims of the institutions, and hence, that critical decisions must continually be made as to the best allocation of these to meet society's needs.

There is no question that the current adequacy of support for education is a matter of great concern, involving reappraisals of present practices by groups ranging from local citizens' committees to the United States Senate, and pertaining both to public schools (e.g., C-4) and to institutions of higher learning (e.g., C-3). Much of this concern has come from research of several kinds indicating that unless fundamental changes are made in the bases of support for education in our society the educational system will not be able to meet the demands which society places on it.

Thus, the demographic studies of the past ten years, describing the increases in the population of student age and projecting further increases in future years, force the conclusion that facilities for education will have to be greatly expanded, and those for higher education in particular nearly doubled, if the educational institution is to meet society's demands.

A second body of research has described the failure to recruit able students into higher educational systems, and shows the substantial loss to society through its failure to educate its native talent so that it can make contributions to the adult social order. An excellent summary of the many researches pertaining to talent loss is available (C-7). A series of studies dating from the work of Sibley (E-18) and continuing through the past decade are reported in detail in the next section. They are pertinent here in indicating that though recruitment involves not just monetary matters, yet a large number of able persons wishing to continue their education are unable to do so because of lack of money. This work has already resulted in visible changes in allocation of resources to education, namely, the very rapid increase of scholarships, their value having doubled during the past five years to the current level of $66 million annually. Notwithstanding this rapid increase, there are still far too few to meet the higher educational needs of all able students. Proportionately, the problem is still a major one.

Still another type of research has dealt with the inability of the education system to retain its teachers, once it has recruited them. As many as one-third of all persons trained in education do not enter the field, and no more than two-fifths of those prepared are at any one time actually teaching (D-17: Chapter 18; D-21). In some major part this is a result of low salaries. The data presented in Lieberman (C-2) and especially the recent report by Ruml and Tickton (C-5) describe the decline in real purchasing power of educational groups over the past fifty years, and show this decline to be pronounced at the higher levels of status.

What line of research might the sociologist undertake in addition to those noted above? It would appear that he might strike as close to the heart of the allocation problem as he can, and recognizing the importance of social values and social power in the matter, undertake studies of their role in, their influence upon, the allocation process.

The wishes of the individual member of society as to how he would distribute his resources is dependent on his order of preference for one or another institutionalized activity. The family budget, for example, contains the manifestation of this ordering of desires. Where education ranks in the individual's value system, and how this varies from time to time and from group to group, is as yet unstudied. The only related data involve public opinion samples. Brookover (F-4) has summarized certain data from public opinion polls since the mid-1940's. It indicates that the public would support the allocation of greater funds to their schools, and that the majority of respondents believe that teachers are underpaid. More detailed findings come from the national high school sample of the Purdue Public Opinion Poll (B-16), reporting an increase over the past years in percentage of high school students who believe teachers are underpaid, and showing, in addition, that the percentage of students who believe this is positively correlated with the students' socioeconomic level.

The fact is, of course, that the allocation process is governed by a number of groups, with varying degrees of power, who will customarily possess different sets of values, or at least different rankings of values. Thus, for some groups education is preferred to national defense, to road construction, or to recreational facilities. For other groups this is not the case. The final decisions are those made by the individuals invested by society with the responsibility for the institutionalized area of education. Hence, the research problem leads directly to studies of such matters as the values held by school board members, by state boards of regents, and the like; to the process through which persons representing one or another set of interests are placed in such positions of public trust; to the manner in which conflicting interests within such a group are resolved. These and related questions await attention.

### Allocation to Different Educational Systems

Turning now to the question of allocation between educational systems, the important contributions of sociology in this area lie in the research describing the differential allocation of resources to educational institutions contingent on the clientele which they serve. Opening with the work of Gunnar Myrdal and continuing through the influential work of Warner, Havighurst, and Loeb (C-6) up to the recent past, for example, the summary materials by Ashmore (C-1) on race, the research has documented the unequal distribution of resources for education in accord with the race and social class of the school population; and has shown a greater allocation for education where the institutions serve white, middle, and upper-class groups. Where the aims of education are, in fact, different for different class and racial groups, then differential allocation flows legitimately from such aims. Where, however, it is held that the aims of education should not be differentiated on the basis of social origin, but solely on the basis of ability, if at all, the research shows a discriminatory allocation of society's resources.

It was this research, combined with studies from other disciplines documenting that prejudice and discrimination are learned and that ability differences are not related to the genetic aspects of race, which provided the scientific support for the recent federal action against segregation in public education. The work done in this area can stand as one of the significant contributions of sociology and goes far to make up for the relative absence of interest in education during the late 1930's and 1940's.

### Allocation Within a System

With respect to allocation of resources within a single educational organization, apparently no research in the sociological tradition has been made. A number of problems command one's interest here. One in particular would seem to lie squarely within the sociological study of occupations, namely, the basis of differences in salaries and rates of occupational advancement.

Talcott Parsons has made a distinction between two types of individual characteristics, namely, qualities such as age, sex, training, social origins, and behavioral attributes or performance. It is probable that all organizations employ both of these as criteria in rewarding their personnel. However, different institutions will emphasize one to the detriment of the other.

Education at the lower levels is increasingly characterized by the use of quality criteria, namely, amount of training, longevity, and sex, in contrast to performance criteria such as success in teaching or ratings of competence by one's peers. In this regard it is quite similar to governmental institutions, at least where nonelective positions are concerned. Why should this be true of these two institutions, while a business firm stresses the opposite type of criteria? Are performance criteria employed in society only where merit is easily assessable? All will recognize that higher education can lay much greater stress upon performance, and does so, since the number and length of a professor's publications is highly objective. Elementary and secondary school teachers in contrast are not expected to publish learned articles. One would argue that if college professors were to be rated on their performance in the classroom, the use of quality criteria would increase in universities.

The issue does not end there. What might the effects be on other aspects of the institution of the lack of stress on performance? Is it not likely that persons who stress self-sufficiency, competition, and individual achievement will seek occupations other than teaching? Does the lack of stress on performance become transmitted to the students, thereby affecting their own performances? Enough natural differences exist in the schools today with respect to their emphasis upon quality or performance to justify research here.

Thus, this simple difference in the basis of allocation of rewards within the school system seems not so simple, but rather to relate to some fundamental aspects of social organization, and truly begs for the attention of social scientists.

# IV

# THE ALLOCATION OF PERSONNEL: THE EDUCATORS

IN THIS SECTION we consider the research on the broad question of how teaching personnel are recruited into and are advanced through different positions in the educational institution. The sociologist would view this as part of the broad process of societal distribution of personnel into positions in the social structure, a process traditionally studied by the divisions of sociology concerned with occupations and with social stratification.

## Recruitment

With respect, first, to the issue of recruitment, data are available on several characteristics of the persons who enter teaching. One must be mindful of Lieberman's caution, however, in his excellent review of this area (C-2), that it is hazardous to generalize for a group of over one million teachers, and that ideally all findings should be qualified by region, age, school level, and the like.

Most of the studies of class origin, dating from the basic work of Greenhoe (D-7) in 1941 and including excellent recent work such as Terrien's (D-18) are reviewed in the basic references we have cited before (D-4, D-8). In light of our prior caution, and of studies (e.g., C-6, D-17: Chapter 2) indicating that teacher class origins will vary depending on the city or region, any conclusions must be viewed as tentative. With these limitations, one can state that the research supports the conclusion that the preponderance of elementary and secondary school teachers come from lower-middle-class backgrounds. This is increasingly true, for the comparison of recent with earlier surveys shows a clear change in this direction, and age comparisons (D-17: Chapter 2) show the younger teacher to have come much more frequently from labor-class origins.

With regard to the differential recruitment of men and women, one notes that more than 90 per cent of all elementary school teachers are women, and the percentages for secondary and higher education are 60 and 25 per cent, respectively. All these percentages are higher than in any other country, and this distribution has persisted for a long time (C-2).

These two sets of data suggest how society is able to recruit teachers in spite of the low salary scale, when they are considered in conjunction with research findings on the prestige of teaching, and the career plans of women teachers. First, studies of the prestige rankings of occupations (e.g., D-13) show teaching below the college level to be not far above the average for all occupations. The critical point, though, is that it is in fact above the average and especially that it outranks blue-collar occupations. Moreover, a recent study (D-14) shows that the amount of prestige accorded by college students to teaching is negatively correlated with their own social class position, higher prestige being assigned to teaching by students from lower-class groups. These facts strongly suggest that the common motive for entering teaching may be to move up in the social scale, and that this may be increasing in importance. Second, the research (D-10: pp. 252–253), showing that some three-fourths of women teachers under thirty (whether married or single) wish to be housewives ten years later, indicates teaching to be for many women a temporary activity, providing a socially acceptable niche until the occasions of marriage and motherhood.

One might suppose that recruitment into an occupation through motives such as these would lead to frequent changes and loss of personnel. The data reported in the previous section on the low proportions of trained teachers who are at any one time actually teaching, and the additional work of Charters (D-6) on this problem suggest that this is the case. How the rate of turnover compares to other occupational groups is not clear, however. While it seems unlikely that for other professions as many as one-third of the trained personnel are not actually practicing, further work comparing different occupations in this respect seems advisable.

The issue of turnover rates leads directly to a question with both practical and theoretical overtones, namely, how to select for the various occupations those persons with the lowest risk of turnover. Charters points out that with respect to education men and career-oriented women would be better risks than the traditionally oriented women. One can also hypothesize that recruitment among men of those with lower-class backgrounds and strong social mobility desires would assure greater continuity in the occupation than selection of men less concerned with mobility, or who come from a status already equivalent in prestige with the occupation of teaching.

Turning now to consideration of the many studies on personality characteristics of educators which are designed to see if education recruits a special type of personality, comprehensive reviews (D-10) show no systematic commonality of interests or other traits among educators. One might consider as the one exception the data reported by Wolfle (D-21) on intelligence. These show the average intelligence of college graduates and graduate students entering the teaching profession to be below the average for all professions, ranking fifteenth out of nineteen major professional fields, and followed in order by dentistry, business and commerce, home economics, and physical education. Note that this does not mean that education does not recruit as many persons, in absolute numbers, of high level ability, but rather that it also must recruit very heavily from the less able groups in order to reach its current personnel quota of a million and more individuals.

## Selection

The selection of teachers from among those initially recruited is based on formal certification requirements (D-10: Chapters 4, 6) which specify the type of training necessary for teaching. The implication of selecting educational personnel on the basis of training alone is that educational roles can be performed by persons of any kind, given the specified training. What, then, of the crucial question of whether there are not personal and social characteristics which greatly influence role performance and hence should be employed as selective criteria?

The failure in education to use such criteria in selecting personnel does not arise from ignorance of this possibility. The fact is, on the contrary, that continuing attention has been given to the problem of finding suitable criteria, that is, personal and social criteria which are related to success in the educational role. However, even though there is a vast body of research on the relation of teacher characteristics to effectiveness in teaching, the reviews of this research (D-15, D-1) show no consistent relation between any characteristics, including intelligence, and such teaching effectiveness.

While the importance of this conclusion for education is great, its implications for sociology loom even larger. Can these results mean what they seem to, that training in method together with the actual demands of the role are sufficient to overcome all measurable effects of personal and idiosyncratic characteristics of the teacher upon the effectiveness of his performance? If true, this is a social science finding of more than educational importance, and clearly demands the further consideration of sociologists.

Perhaps the effects of the teacher's personality have been looked for in the wrong place; perhaps it is not with respect to the student's academic learning that such effects occur, but rather with respect to other outcomes of the educational process, namely, the kind of values the student learns, his feelings about himself and other persons, his attitudes toward further education, and many other matters. Research which focused on these latter results of education and related them to types of teacher personalities might well discover some effects of teacher characteristics upon the products of education which are of cardinal importance.

Of equal likelihood, and indeed, as a major proposition from sociological theory, is the possibility that the influence of a teacher's characteristics upon his effectiveness as an educator is contingent on characteristics of the students. Some teachers of given personal characteristics may be more effective with boys, others with girls; some with bright children, others with the average student; some may work best with the social isolates, others with the classroom leaders; some may teach best the working-class youngsters, while others do better with the middle-class students. Teachers themselves are the first to admit that they seem to do better with one rather than another type of student, and the preferences of different students for various teachers is easily recognized as part of one's own life experience. This is not, therefore, a novel observation, but somehow it seems to have escaped attention as a critical research problem. Were the sociologist to dig in here and analyze the interpersonal relations between various types of teachers and students, correlating these with educational results, the results of his study could point the way toward selecting teachers of certain characteristics to work with certain types of children. In any event it would be a move away from the stultifying conception of some single optimum type of teacher, which one tries to produce through training, and to which one demands the conformity of all educational personnel. At the same time, and it hardly seems necessary to mention, such research would contribute to sociology a greater understanding of its core problem, the relative determining power over human interaction of personal and social factors.

### Career Patterns

The study of the career patterns of educators is relatively undeveloped although within the past half-dozen years the research has increased in volume. With respect to elementary and secondary school educators, there have been a series of doctoral theses completed at the University of Chicago which together with related research are summarized in the recent general text of Havighurst and Neugarten (D-8: Chapter 19). Noteworthy among available research is Becker's analysis (D-2, D-3) of the two different paths of mobility followed by educational personnel. One is a horizontal mobility path in which the educator seeks positions in school systems preferred on the basis of type of pupil, location, age of children being taught, type of subject, and the like, salary not being a dominant factor in this choice. The other is a traditional vertical mobility path in which one moves up through higher levels of administrative status. The latter is much more often taken by men (D-17: Chapter 18) and here income seems to play a larger role in determining the desirability of the position, Mason and Gross (D-11) finding that salary alone correlates .89 with prestige ranking of different school superintendents' positions.

The most important work currently available on higher education career matters is Woodburne's definitive analysis (D-20) of personnel policies of forty-six leading colleges and universities. The author reports on a series of topics including appointments, promotions, salary practices, teaching and research, terms of appointment, separation from the institution, conditions of work, leaves of absence, and tenure and retirement. The analysis leads to a series of observations which should be of central interest to the sociologist making comparative studies of occupational patterns. For example, he points out that the greatest difficulty to the institution occurs with respect to separating (firing, not renewing an appointment, and the like) a teacher from the college. With respect to tenure, he observes that while it functions in the traditional matter to protect freedom of thought, it is dysfunctional for obtaining the best possible faculty, in that permanent appointments are given before suitable evaluation of merit can be made. It appears that this report is too little known to sociologists. One might add that it is of personal interest in its own right to the university teacher, apart from its contribution to the study of education, and that for the graduate student it stands as an important guide to the academic life.

Some earlier studies have dealt intensively with several of the matters discussed in Woodburne's report. Hollingshead's research (D-9) on progression through faculty ranks describes average lengths of time spent in the various ranks and other aspects of the mobility pattern. Sorokin (D-16) has summarized a study he made more than twenty-five years ago of patterns of faculty recruitment in four major universities. He reports among other things that recruitment into the professor and associate professor ranks is more frequently from the lower ranks at the same university than it is from outside sources, thereby indicating that the most probable path to a tenure appointment at a university is to join the university at an early stage of one's career and to stay there. One wonders if this is still true today. Our knowledge of these matters will be brought up to date by the forthcoming book by Caplow and McGee (D-5), presenting the results of an extensive study of faculty mobility within and between ten major American universities.

The review would not be complete without inclusion of Logan Wilson's *The Academic Man* (D-19) which, though not systematic research in the sense that the above-mentioned studies are, is a sensitive and insightful description of the career and problems of the university professor and has served many classes of graduate students as a primary source of information about the life which lies ahead for them.

The paucity of our knowledge of the career of the educator at these higher levels is the more surprising since the matter lies so close at hand. As someone has said, university faculties know more about anything else one could name than they do about themselves and their natural habitat. Questions both fascinating (because of their relevance to one's own career) and theoretically important exist in abundance here, and have the further characteristic of being accessible to study. To pick up the observation of Woodburne, one might wish to inquire further into the functions of tenure for an institutional system. There seems to have been no sociological study of tenure, nor any comparative analysis made of the effects of this type of status on different institutional processes. One might well ask why other major institutions have no need of tenure positions, or whether they in fact do not have their functional equivalent under another name. Or, to take another example, is higher education the only institutional area in which one must move either up or out, so that there are no lifetime assistant professors? Is this necessary to make room to train new men at lower levels for recruitment into the higher echelons, or is its more important function that of eliciting a maximum achievement effort from the younger recruits? How do other institutions deal with this issue?

# V

# THE ALLOCATION OF PERSONNEL: THE STUDENTS

WHEN IN A COMPLEX CULTURE it is necessary to establish a separate formal institution of education, society is faced with the problems of recruitment of its children into this system, of selection of children for different kinds and amounts of education, and of advancing them according to some pattern through successive levels of educational attainment.

## Recruitment

The basic social solution of the recruitment problem has been the development of compulsory education, dating from the first part of the eighteenth century in Germany. While this method works to maintain by law membership in the institution, it leaves several aspects of the problem unresolved. One is that it is differentially successful in this country, depending on geographical region, and on the age, sex, race, and residence of the children. In a recent volume (E-4), one of a series of monographs utilizing the 1950 census data which are sponsored by the Social Science Research Council, Eleanor Bernert has reported on educational characteristics of American children. The data pertain to children up to the age of twenty. Three characteristics are considered: attendance by year of school; number of years completed; and age-grade progress, that is, whether the student is above or below his expected grade in school on the basis of his age. The data show in general that among female, white, urban, nonsouthern, and younger children, there is a higher percentage who are students.

Compulsory education leaves unresolved several other aspects of recruitment. The first is motivation for adequate role performance in the system, for example, applying oneself to one's studies. The second is the related problem of the handling and disposition of those students who refuse to perform an acceptable role in the system; this is considered in another section in connection with the role of the educator. Third, the problem remains of recruitment into the higher levels of education which society feels are desirable, but not yet so important as to be made compulsory.

In the area of student recruitment the research of sociologists has been outstanding. A series of notable studies recently summarized by Havighurst and Neugarten (E-8: pp. 226–228) have demonstrated what is now referred to as talent loss. This loss occurs both from a less than optimal performance in the educational system, and from the student's failure to continue advanced educational training beyond that which is required.

Accepting the fact that the intelligence of the student is one important determinant of recruitment into the higher educational systems, these studies have shown that when intelligence is controlled, there is still an important variation in recruitment resulting from the effects of the social class and ethnic background of the students. An excellent review of the research on high school dropouts (E-1) supports this conclusion. With respect to higher education, research by Sibley (E-18) shows that both the high school student's intelligence and his father's occupation are related to the amount of education he will obtain; namely, that as both rise, the chances of his completing higher grades of education increase; but notably that his intelligence is more closely related to his educational attainment at the secondary level or below, and that for achievement in higher education his father's occupation is a better predictor than is his own intelligence.

The facilitating effect of higher social status on educational attainment occurs in the large follow-up study of gifted children by Terman and Oden (E-20). The fact that in this case the effect of social status on education holds for persons whose average intelligence is over 150 suggests the power of social-class membership. This study also shows differential achievement by ethnicity, with a comparatively smaller loss of talent occurring among Jews in comparison with other ethnic groups.

At first glance the obvious explanation would seem to be that failure of lower-status students to be recruited in accordance with their ability is attributable to lack of money. This is to some extent true, and as we have said provides the justification for scholarships to needy students. However, the pivotal studies by Mulligan (E-14, E-15) show that under the G.I. Bill of Rights students from semi-skilled and unskilled social backgrounds, though increasing their proportionate representation at Indiana University, still did not take full advantage of this opportunity for higher education in proportion to their numbers.

Further documentation of the fact that economic hardship alone does not explain talent loss is provided in studies comparing religious or ethnic groups of the same class level. Mulligan shows that the religious representation at the University of working-class groups, computed on the basis of an estimate of their absolute numbers in the state, ranges from 1 per cent of the Catholics to 61 per cent of the Jews, with the Protestants falling in the middle. The forthcoming publication by Baldwin and others (E-3) includes data showing the superior educational attainment of Jews in contrast to Italian Catholics of the same economic level.

The above-mentioned studies deal with differential recruitment by class and ethnic background where economic and/or intellectual level are controlled. Are there subcultural differences in values which might explain this? The answer is unequivocally yes. The national survey data on values reported by Hyman (E-11), and the data reported in the forthcoming volume on talent development mentioned above (E-3) show a greater value placed on higher education by higher, as contrasted with lower, classes and by Jews in contrast to Catholics. In addition, the series of studies by Sewell and his associates (e.g., E-17) are especially valuable in that they first control for intelligence, and then show that for high school students educational aspiration still rises with social status. Other data from this research program show that among nonfarm and farm boys who are equated in intelligence, the former have higher educational aspirations.

The Department of Social Relations at Harvard has for several years been engaged in a study of social mobility, including educational attainment. The results are anticipated with interest, since the project seeks to relate educational aspirations to very general value differences. Preliminary reports of the data show that the values of subcultural groups relating to education may be transmitted to the child as early as the elementary school period.

Two other studies have attempted to refine the analysis of value differences by examining intragroup variations, on the one hand, and by a more careful conceptualization of the actual values, on the other. Kahl (E-12) has studied the differences in educational aspiration of children within the same social group. Contrasting boys of high and low educational ambition who have similar intelligence and similar low family status, he shows that parents of the ambitious boys were not content with their current class and that they tended to train their sons from earliest years to use education as a means to climb into the middle class. This suggests that a high value is placed on education by the less well-recruited groups, but not to the extent found, say, in middle-class and Jewish groups.

Rosen (E-16) first distinguishes between the criteria of successful recruitment, namely, performance level and attainment level, then makes the distinction between achievement motivation and achievement-oriented values. Examining the relation between performance, attainment, motivation and values, he demonstrates that achievement motivation is related to marks achieved in school, whereas the achievement values are related to educational aspiration (desire to go to college). These results hold across classes, and within each class separately; however, consistent with the research mentioned above, he finds that while both high achievement motivation and high achievement values do occur in lower-class groups, both are more commonly associated with high social status.

A somewhat different question about recruitment is that of the personal and social characteristics of student's attending different kinds of schools and colleges. This is to date a comparatively unexplored field, yet the work done already has turned up some most interesting student differences.

For the secondary school level McArthur (E-13) has shown in a review of his own and other research that there are some significant differences in behavior and personality between public and private school boys. The former are clearer about their occupational career, achieve higher grades in college, and are more concerned with their performance than with the personal qualities or attributes they possess.

For the higher education level, Havighurst and Neugarten (E-8) using several sources have estimated the social class composition of the student body in various types of higher institutions such as universities, small liberal arts colleges, and Ivy League schools. The results seem to fit what one would expect on the basis of social class predictions and residential propinquity.

With reference to differential recruitment on the basis of ability, Holland (E-9) has reported on the college choice of a large sample of highly able students (the top 5 per cent of secondary school graduates). Holland uses the list of colleges and universities developed by Knapp and his colleagues (H-8, H-9), which presents a ranking according to their rate of production of eminent scientists. He then shows that occupation of the student's father is significantly related to the selection of a high-productivity institution. The relation, however, is not with the level of occupation, but with its type. Those students who significantly more often select colleges with high productivity rates have fathers who work with their hands, with scientific ideas, or with people in a social service sense, in contrast to students whose fathers' work is characterized by "oral persuasive" or leadership activities, especially in supervisory and government positions. Why this is so is difficult to say, but it should be followed up, for it certainly indicates significant differences in values among groups of occupations and suggests that there exists a more powerful theoretical classification of values than one based on social class.

### Selection

Turning now to the second issue in the allocation of student personnel, namely, selection of students for different types and amounts of education, one recognizes that the initial selection of students is based almost wholly on chronological age. Progression through the institution to different statuses continues to be dependent in part on age, but both personal qualities and role performance criteria gain importance as bases of selection. Scholastic achievement, intelligence test performance, sex, race, religion, and social class, to name but a few, are intermingled in varying combinations as criteria for selection into higher grades and into colleges and universities. Some conception of the variety of criteria, formal and informal, which are used for selecting college students is obtained from a report of the American Council on Education (E-2).

In this area a continuing research program at the University of Chicago has produced work (E-5, E-6) critical of the probable bias in tests of intellectual ability, pointing out that the items used in intelligence tests are drawn from middle-class experience and hence discriminate against lower-status groups. The program has produced new tests of ability presumably consisting of culture-free, hence unbiased, items. A recognized difficulty here is that in a real sense it is impossible to demonstrate that class differences on test items result from "bias" or from "innate differences." One criticism has been that through removing those items on which class differences exist, and for which a seemingly legitimate case for bias can be made, true differences in intelligence may in fact be masked. Another line of criticism, with a more practical orientation, is that one should not pursue the issue of innate differences but should recognize that intelligence must be defined in terms of ability to meet the problems presented by the environment. In this sense a biased test is nevertheless a valid measure of lower-class ability to meet middle-class problems, and to the extent that the school emphasizes such problems, it is therefore a valid criterion for selection of students.

Other studies have explored the effect of student social class upon informal selection procedures. Hollingshead (E-10) in particular has shown that with students of equal ability but of varying class the teacher favors for educational advancement the higher-class student, and implements this selection through recommendations, course grading, assignment to college preparatory courses, scholarship awards, and the like. However, Hollingshead's work is based on a small static community and few replications of this study have been made. One can recognize that in other types of communities, for example, Chicago or New York, this generalization might not hold. In any case, the implications of Hollingshead's findings are of such basic importance that their validity should be tested in different kinds of social environments.

Race is a criterion of assigning students to different schools in many communities. The current desegregation of the schools can thus be viewed as a change in the criteria and processes used in selecting students. This change has made the schools a natural laboratory for research on intra-institutional relations, that is, for studies of the effect of changes in personnel selection upon other elements such as aims, role prescriptions, and functions. A group of studies has been presented by Williams and Ryan (E-21) which suggest the effects of such institutional change. The publication prepared by the Cornell group (E-19) formalizes research propositions in this area and describes the contributions which sociologists are in a position to make.

Much awaits the result of sociological labor on the general process of selection in the schools. Just two instances of possible research on the effects of certain selection criteria might be given. First, no comparative study yet exists of the effect upon students of attending a same-sex as opposed to a mixed-sex school or college. It would seem that two boys, one spending fifteen years of his school life with only his own sex, the other attending coeducational schools for the same period, would differ in significant ways upon graduation. At the least it seems a hypothesis worthy of test.

Second, what might be the effects upon students' attitudes toward competition, toward intellectual endeavor, and toward democratic values of being members of a school which segregates students into classes differentiated by intellectual ability, in contrast to establishing classes so that each includes a wide variation in intelligence and other types of abilities. This is the perennial question of the merits of ability grouping, once again in the public arena. Even after a generation of educational trial and error, with much argument pro and con, it is startling to find that the basic studies of the effects of such grouping on student attitudes and self-concepts remain to be done. With respect to academic performance, if it is found that heterogeneous ability groupings of students produce peer group norms of conformity to the average, of regression to the mean of academic achievement, whereas homogeneous groupings produce norms supporting individual achievement, and if it is further shown that such norms are strong enough to encourage or reduce academic effort, then where education stresses academic achievement the appropriate process for student allocation is clear. To be sure, aims other than academic achievement may thus be forfeited. In any case, a decision between aims is forced. The functions of research in clarifying problems, in documenting inherent conflicts in the educational system which currently can be glossed over in the absence of data, and in thus finally forcing a rational decision based on scientific materials, are exemplified in this critical problem.

### The Pattern of Advancement

The student moves through a series of graded positions with little choice on his own part as to their sequence. The natural or experimental variations in the normal pattern of advancement for students have been few in number, and have attracted little research attention. The experimental project of the Fund for the Advancement of Education, moving able students on to college before termination of high school, has been evaluated and described in a recent work (E-7). The results show that the advanced students did as well in college work as comparable regularly enrolled college students did. However, the data are not adequate to answer some of the central questions one would want to raise about the program; for example, in what ways do the students involved differ as a result of this novel educational career pattern from equivalent students who were not advanced.

In many educational systems children may skip grades or be held back a year. The merits of this procedure, as was true with respect to ability groupings, have been debated for many years, yet systematic studies of the effects of the procedure, other than academic performance, remain to be made. To put the problem more generally, age-grading is a fundamental aspect of society, and progression through educational and occupational roles is ordinarily consonant with the attainment of certain age grades. On the other hand, certain individuals will be advanced or retarded with respect to their age peers in their advancement through different positions. What are the major consequences of such variations, both for the individual and for those with whom he is associated in school or work, for example, upon one's feelings of self-worth, his attitudes toward high achievement, or his isolation from others?

# VI

# ROLES IN THE INSTITUTION: THE EDUCATORS

A BRIEF CONSIDERATION of two general points of theory helps to frame the discussion of research which follows. The first point is that role prescriptions for educators, as for the personnel in all institutions, are based upon beliefs which relate role behavior in the institution to the successful achievement of aims set for the institution. It follows that differences in role prescriptions for educators, whether between members of the public or the educators themselves, may arise from differences in aims, or from differences in beliefs about how to achieve what are actually the same aims. Thus, one would expect to find in comparisons of parochial, private, and public schools that the role expected of the educator will differ because the systems have different aims. So, too, one would expect to find in comparisons of persons holding various theories of human nature and learning, for example, a Calvinist versus a Freudian, a follower of Rousseau versus a student of Dewey, that their prescriptions for the educator's role would be radically different, even though they may share the same ideal for the person to be developed through education. Without exception, the research reviewed below describing differences in role expectations has failed to differentiate the sources of the differences into either conflicting aims or theories of behavior.

The second general point pertains to public versus institutional control over role performance. This issue lies at the center of the problem of whether education is in fact a profession. Where education is regarded as a profession, the aims of the institution will be set by the society at large and society will reserve the right to

45

evaluate the degree of success in the achievement of such aims, that is, to assess the actual functions performed by the institution. However, the selection of means (role behavior) to achieve the aims is seen as a technical matter, requiring special training, and will be left to the institutional personnel themselves. In this case education is comparable to medicine and the law, where the aims are drawn from and their achievement evaluated by the larger society, but where the physician and lawyer possess the right to pursue them in the light of their superior knowledge, regulated only by their own colleagues.

The fact is that the public still claims the right to prescribe the roles of educators, even though we know little what the actual prescriptions are. Educators may consider themselves to be professionals, but sectors of the public have not yet granted this status. Conflict is experienced by teachers (F-10) in that while they are expected to be experts in their particular fields, nevertheless community groups dictate educational practices, such as the marking system and the amount of assigned homework, which they must follow, and which at times are contrary to their expert judgment.

Why should this plight beset the educators? Is it because society's members themselves have strong personal convictions about how children learn, based on their experiences as parents; or that the scientific basis of educational theory is negligible, at least in the eyes of the parents, so that one man's opinion equals another's? Or is it because the proof of superiority of one method over another is too difficult to demonstrate to the public, unlike medicine where the patient improves or declines? Or, finally, is it that the public distrusts the educators, feeling that new aims are being smuggled in under the guise of professional methods, so that the public recourse is to prescribe the methods themselves? Somewhere in here lies an important truth and the sociologist who successfully threads his way through the problem will make a basic contribution to the comparative study of the professions, as well as to the public welfare.

It has seemed in our overview of research on roles that the data fall into groups pertaining to the educator's roles in the classroom, with his colleagues, and in the community. There are, in addition, some general treatments of educator roles not specific to any of these three contexts. These include Willard Waller's *The Sociology of Teaching* (F-31), a pioneer descriptive study of the school which emphasizes the roles of the teacher, and Logan Wilson's work, mentioned earlier (F-32), describing the role of the college professor. The forthcoming study by Lazarsfeld and Thielens (F-21) is based on a national sample of social scientists' descriptions of their behavior under pressures to conform in institutions of higher education and will augment our knowledge of the college teacher.

### Roles in the Classroom: Prescriptive Aspects

Considering first the educators' prescriptions for themselves, the basic data are found in standard general works on educational curriculum and method (e.g., F-7, F-26). Two points seem pertinent: the first is that the variety of procedures suggested by such work indicates underlying differences both in aims of education and in theories of how to achieve them. To the degree that the latter obtains, it reflects the fact that the scientific support of such theories, namely, the findings of the behavior sciences, is not well developed. The second point is that examination will show the educational theories underlying such role prescriptions to be almost totally devoid of sociological principles, and to draw instead almost wholly on individual psychology.

With respect to role prescriptions by students for educators in the classroom, a number of studies have been made over the years. Considering this work as a whole, a significant theme seems to pertain to the instrumental-expressive dichotomy between roles in small groups. Research on small groups has shown that groups tend to develop at least two "leaders," one being instrumental or task oriented, the other being expressive or concerned with the feelings or social-emotional concerns of group members. It is suggested that both the task and the members' feelings must be attended to, and that a division of labor seems to arise. It is further shown that the task leader is respected for his contribution, but that the expressive leader is the better liked. One may thus ask how the teacher handles these two demands in his solitary position as a group leader.

Studies of different kinds throw light on this issue. Brookover (F-6: Chapter 9), reviewing the informal evidence on teacher roles in the school, suggests that in the teacher's relation to the pupils the expected role is that of dominance and social distance. This evidence, however, seems to be specific neither to the level of the school, e.g., high school or college, nor to the type of school, e.g., progressive versus traditional. Other studies, such as the extensive research by Riley and his colleagues (F-24) on student attitudes toward college teachers, as well as the dozen or so studies of student ratings of college teachers which they review, show the student to favor teacher characteristics of a more expressive kind. In particular, this study shows that the preferential rank order of qualities of teachers are knowledge of subject matter, a sympathetic attitude, and interest in subject, with the bottom ranks comprising good speaking ability, clear explanation, and fairness. Moreover, the two major surveys of student attitudes, the Cornell study (F-28) and the Purdue research (F-22), both report a large percentage of students wishing their teachers took more personal interest in them, or were more friendly and sympathetic. Finally, the study by Jenkins and Lippitt (F-19) shows that teachers wish to be more friendly and personal and that students underestimate the extent to which they desire this.

Closely related also are reports (F-4, F-5) of a notable study by Brookover dealing with actual classroom performance. Sixty-six high school history teachers are classified as primarily authoritarian or democratic (congenial, friendly, sympathetic). One needs to assume here that the authoritarian teacher is more task-oriented, more concerned with academic matters in the classroom, while the democratic teacher, as described, gives relatively more attention to social-emotional concerns. Brookover finds in this study that the authoritarian teachers are more respected by their students, but less well liked; that students of these teachers learned more history; and that in the school either role may be equally "acceptable," but failure to perform adequately in one or the other leads to censure.

With the qualification that the findings may be true only for certain kinds of educational systems, this group of studies points to several things: that the dominant role prescription for teachers is to be task-oriented, though either role is acceptable; that teachers follow this at the expense of expressive considerations; that they gain respect but lose attraction in doing this; that both teacher and student wish more attention were (or could be) given to expressive or social-emotional matters, and, finally, that if they do, learning (or task accomplishment) suffers. This all suggests that the demands that the teacher in the classroom handle both instrumental and expressive aspects of the leadership role by himself are incompatible, and that further analysis of types of solutions and their consequences are of interest both to education and to small group theory.

One other stimulating finding has emerged from research on classroom role prescriptions by students. In the study by Riley and others mentioned above, the results show that the great majority of the teachers were enthusiastic over hearing what students think of their behavior and in learning how the students wish them to behave. In an unpublished study by Daniel Price of the University of North Carolina, a similar finding occurred, with a retest showing teachers to have made significant changes in the direction of student prescription. This suggests that the college teacher, at least, has been protected from reciprocity in the teacher-student relation to a degree which leaves him uncomfortable and motivated to discover what the other person in the relation feels about his performance.

Prescriptions for the educators' role in the classroom held by a third group, the members of the community, have been studied by Gross (F-14) in a comparison of superintendent prescriptions for classroom procedures with those of members of the press. The items on which they are compared are unrelated and point to no overall conclusion, but they do illustrate the marked disagreements which research can discover. For example, on the fundamental question of whether students should be graded on the basis of their own individual capacity, or graded with respect to uniform standards, 83 per cent of the superintendents and 48 per cent of the press favor the former; the latter is favored by 13 per cent of superintendents and 41 per cent of the press.

Other data on role prescriptions for teachers held by the public are presented in Richey and Fox (F-23), and in the recent doctoral dissertations cited in the reviews by Hines and Curran (F-17) and by Kreitlow (F-20). The data pertain to unrelated aspects of the teacher role and the facts are not organized by theoretical concepts, hence do not lend themselves to summary here. However, the sociologist with a research interest in the teacher's role will want to familiarize himself with this work.

### Roles in the Classroom: Performance Aspects

Several investigators have chosen to study actual classroom performance in contrast to the studies of role expectations cited above. We do not consider here the variety of studies which have conceptualized performance variations in simple psychological terms, for example, the teacher motivating the child through interest, or those which have sought to evaluate the effects of such teaching methods. This research is covered in standard publications on educational psychology such as the recent text by Cronbach (F-9). We refer instead to the studies (few in number) which have examined classroom role performance from a sociological perspective.

The effects of social class of both student and teacher have been explored in several works. Gross has presented a penetrating review and critique (F-13) of these studies. Hollingshead's work (F-18), previously cited, shows that the behavior of high school teachers varies with the social class of the student in such matters as giving grades, recommendations for awards or scholarships, and encouragement in college preparatory courses. Becker (F-2) has shown how the behavior of the teacher with respect to disciplinary and other matters is influenced by the perceived social class of the student. Other social class studies have also stressed these points, though with less documentation.

The classification of role performances along the dimension of authoritarian-democratic behavior has also received attention. Brookover's study of the role performance of high school history teachers has already been discussed and the implications drawn. The influential monographs by Anderson and his colleagues (F-1) describe the effects on the child of such variations in the teacher's classroom behavior. Teachers who dominate produce noncooperating and conflicting responses to them in their pupils, and also tend to induce dominant relations between the students themselves. Teachers whose role performance tends to be integrative and cooperative produce the opposite effect. The impressive longitudinal finding of this research is that in a subsequent year the new students who enter the classes of these teachers adopt the same behavior as did the previous classes, whereas the previous classes which now have moved on to new teachers show almost no correlation between their behavior in the prior classroom and in the new classroom.

A closer examination of specific teacher-pupil interaction has been attempted in other research. Gronlund (F-12) has demonstrated that teachers' preferences for having children in their classes are positively correlated with the pupil being highly chosen by his peers. No causal connection is implied, but it raises the question of whether a teacher's perception of, and behavior toward, a specific student is determined by the way the teacher sees other students treat him, or whether the same qualities his peers find attractive are also appealing to the teacher.

A similar interest is shown in Bush's report (F-8) on a continuing research program at Stanford on teacher roles. His data describe variations in teachers' reactions to students contingent on such pupil characteristics as sex, having common interests with the teacher, showing common social beliefs, and others. The work is most provocative with respect to the issue we raised earlier, namely, the desirability of matching types of teachers with types of pupils in terms of personal and social characteristics. It points to research on classroom behavior which the interaction theorist is well equipped to undertake.

One aspect of the teacher's role would appear to be of such general theoretical interest to the sociologist that it merits attention here. We refer to the way the teacher handles the deviant student in the school. The educational system is required to take on all comers, so to speak. Where the source of deviance is actual inability to conform to the student role, stemming from physical defect or inadequate intelligence, the educational system assigns the deviant student to a special school, or at the higher levels of education, is able to select those students who have already indicated their ability to perform the student role. This leaves unanswered, though, the solution to deviant behavior of the able child where the nonconformity springs from unwillingness, from a lack of appropriate role motivation.

How does the teacher handle this type of deviance? One thinks of the earlier dunce cap and stool, and the birch rod for some, where the teacher had to be physically strong enough to master the biggest boy in the classroom or he did not last. Consider the current appeals to the group welfare, the long trip down the corridor to the principal's office, or the fifteen-minute chats with the parents. Consider that some evidence suggests that at the college level some colleges with a more experimental approach to higher education view deviant behavior primarily as "sick" behavior, while the more traditional view it primarily as "bad." The former use psychological and psychiatric services as means of social control while the latter tend to use punitive measures such as suspension and expulsion.

What are the varieties of ways in which teachers handle the deviant child? Do historical changes and current variations in procedure reflect different conceptions of the child's nature? How is the mode of control related to the teacher's personality? Where is the study comparing the success of different types of social control in the classroom? Are some methods more successful with one type of child than another? What are the effects of one or another mode of control upon classroom morale, the child's self concept, his status in his peer group, and the recurrence of his deviant behavior?

In sum, the school classroom would seem to furnish a research setting of the richest kind for the study of the genesis of deviance and the effects of varying types of social control.

## Roles with Colleagues

With respect to the role of the educator with his colleagues, the outstanding research comes from the School Executive Studies at Harvard. Neal Gross and his colleagues have published the first (F-15) of several volumes to come from this research program. This first report utilizes data on the school superintendent's role as a basis for significant developments in formal role theory, and demonstrates the way in which sociological theory can be enriched through the study of one substantive area of education. A second volume (F-16), referred to in an earlier section, will consider specifically the career problems of the school superintendent, the obstacles he faces, and the problems to which he is exposed.

While the first volume does not place primary emphasis on the substantive problem of the superintendent's role, nevertheless, the data are extremely useful. The study reports on both prescriptive and performance aspects of roles for a sample of Massachusetts school superintendents and of school boards. Data include information on the attributes required of superintendents, the areas of role conflict, the modes of resolution of such conflicts, and their effects on career satisfaction. While the data cannot in any sense be summarized here, a few results might be mentioned. For example, the tremendous variation in role prescriptions is shown by the fact that, on a series of items pertaining to areas such as hiring personnel, allocation of one's personal time, salary recommendations, and budget recommendations, there are statistically significant differences between the superintendents and the school board members on three-fifths of the items. The variations within the public itself in prescriptions for the superintendent's role is seen in the fact that some 50 to 90 per cent of the superintendents (depending on the role area) state that they are subjected to conflicting prescriptions by various groups in the community.

Seeman (F-25) in his study of school systems in twenty-six communities also focused on the role of the superintendent, but as prescribed by teachers. The emphasis is the same as that made by Gross and his colleagues, namely, on the conflict which occurs in the prescriptions. Seeman shows that conflict exists between prescriptions on which teachers agree; for example, that the superintendent spend time with the teachers and also strive to obtain higher salaries for them. The conflict is not readily apparent, but the study shows that there is a negative correlation of a significant size between successfully following the two prescriptions and superintendents report that they do not have the time to do both. Conflict within the teacher group also exists; for example, they split almost half and half on their beliefs as to whether the superintendent should invite teachers to his home for social occasions. A third type of conflict occurs between teacher and superintendent; for example, with respect to who should make the final decision on a doubtful student's passing or failing.

The fact that both of these studies show the superintendent's role prescriptions to involve much conflict raises some interesting further points. It suggests either that roles in society normally have what sociologists would describe as a lot of conflict and that they underestimate the degree to which this is a natural state of affairs, or that the superintendent's role is a special type of instance. In either case it leads to further questions such as how conflict is resolved, or why so much conflict exists, or whether the sociologist's analysis of conflict somehow overemphasizes what is actually experienced within the role.

Apart from these studies of the school superintendent, the role of the educator with his colleagues really has been neglected. Brookover (F-6: pp. 196–199), while presenting a case study of clique formation among educators in one school, points out that there are strong informal cliques in every educational institution (including universities) based on age, congeniality, subject matter, and other characteristics, which are powerful determinants of the actual functioning of the educational system and which have been relatively ignored.

Another research area notable by its absence, both for educators and for students as described in the following section, is that of the process of identification with one's role in the educational institution. Becker and Carper (F-3), for example, have dealt with the process of identification with an occupation by graduate students in physiology, philosophy, and engineering, through continuing contact with their colleagues. Very much needed are comparable studies of the way in which the educator, as teacher or administrator in elementary and secondary schools, or as professor at higher educational levels, acquires knowledge of the roles he is to play and incorporates the necessary skills, motives, and ideology as part of his own personality.

### Roles in the Community

With respect to the final issue, the educator's role in the community, the major data come from Greenhoe's study (F-11) reported in 1941. This study describes both the expected and actual limited participation of teachers in economic, political, and other pressure activities; and their major participation in welfare or service programs in the community. A review (F-6) of other material supports this point. However, the more recent study by Terrien (F-29) and the recent doctoral theses reviewed in Stiles (F-27: Chapter 10) suggest that there is less restriction on the teachers' community role than was previously the case. In Terrien's sample of the population of New London, some 80 per cent of the respondents felt teachers could be active politically if they so desired, and more than four-fifths held that the standards of conduct for teachers should not differ from those for any other group of citizens. Indeed, Terrien elsewhere (F-30) reports that the teachers themselves feel that demands for "middle-class morality" put little or no burden upon them. This may be because for many of them such standards are already their own.

This problem of institutional control over one's role in activities outside the institution poses several questions of interest. One notes reports in popular magazines of the increased tendency in business to "own" their executives in all aspects of life, and sees perhaps a decreased tendency of schools' "owning" teachers in this sense. Under what conditions, then, do institutions need to control the outside behavior of their members? With respect to education, the earlier extensive control probably was predicated on the belief that the teacher must show all the virtues, partly to convince the public he accepted them, partly to be a model to the student. What, then, does a declining control mean? Is it a less strong attachment by the public to the traditional values, or does it represent acceptance of a new theory of learning in which the child's imitation or identification is a minor matter, hence, the teacher's model unimportant?

# VII

# ROLES IN THE INSTITUTION: THE STUDENTS

THE MAJOR ISSUES in the study of student roles parallel those for the educator, namely, his relation to teachers in the classroom, his relation to his fellow students, and his relation to the wider community outside the school.

The sociological analysis of student roles has surprisingly neglected the first and third questions, and dealt almost exclusively with the second, the student-to-student relation. The work on students, however, has taken a further step not made in studies of educators, namely, that of studying the reciprocal effects of the classroom and peer group roles.

## Roles in the Classroom

Sociological data applying to role prescriptions in the classroom are almost nonexistent. We know very little that is systematic of what educators believe and virtually nothing of what the students and the public believe the student classroom role should be. Perhaps it needs to be stressed that knowledge of differential role prescriptions, of their relations to both aims and underlying theory, and of their effects, if actually enforced, is a matter of fundamental importance. It is erroneous to view the issue of student role prescription as involving only simple matters such as doing one's assigned work and the like, when in fact the most basic type of cultural values is involved.

As illustration, consider the familiar difference in the expectations that the student should strive to achieve excellence in terms of absolute standards versus the prescriptions that he work up to his personal ability level. How do educators, students, and parents stand on this issue? To what end is the latter prescription directed, that of inner security as contrasted with external achievement? Is the latter prescription supplanting the former; and, if so, with what consequences a generation hence for the traditional upward mobility and high achievement orientation of American culture?

Consider also the differences in expectations that a student be permitted in a schoolroom to express his personal and idiosyncratic desires, to act out, as they say, his inner needs in contrast with the demand that he practice self-discipline and control in relation to social values. Does the former represent a psychiatric approach to human behavior supplanting the Puritan conception? If so, with what consequences for the school system immediately, and the social order later after a generation of children have spent their formative years in this permissive environment?

What is the student expected to do, and how are these expectations distributed among the population? The beliefs of educators concerning how students should behave are the reciprocal of their prescriptions for their own roles in the system, and hence appear most frequently in standard works in educational theory and method. The same points made in the preceding section regarding educators' role prescriptions for themselves are applicable to prescriptions for students also; namely, they are general in nature, they are not codified, their variety indicates variation both in aims and in theories of human (student) behavior; and very little use is made of sociological theory in their formulation.

While many statements attest to the concern of the educators, the statements are not useful as research data in their current form. To our knowledge no one has systematically sampled educators' opinions regarding the desirability of a number of characteristics of the student's role, for example, docility, obedience, level of aspiration, spontaneity, responsibility; nor how these should vary by age, sex, intelligence, and other attributes of the student. While from studies of child-rearing practices we know something of the kind of behavior which parents demand, we never have made studies of the behavior expected in the classroom comparable to these studies of socialization in the home.

There is research (G-20) showing that teachers overestimate the seriousness of traits such as aggressiveness as indicators of a child's maladjustment, and underestimate the seriousness of the child's being quiet and withdrawn; by implication, the latter is viewed by them as more acceptable. In line with this is the provocative observational research by Henry (G-16) reporting that teachers cultivate in their students a docile and acquiescent mode of behavior. These serve to increase one's desire for a major study in this area which would describe the behavior educators prize in children and the way this varies by school and by type of teacher.

When one considers student and community prescriptions for student classroom behavior, the picture is no better. Results from the Purdue Public Opinion Poll (G-22) show among high school students a marked increase in the power they believe they should be given (for example, in student government) as their socio-economic status and class in school increases. The comparison of role prescriptions by school superintendents and the press has already been cited (G-13) and shows the basic disagreements which may exist between the public and educators. Of the items pertaining to the student role in the classroom, the following is an example: with respect to the importance of spontaneity and creativity in the classroom, in contrast to discipline and order, 67 per cent of the superintendents value the former, 26 per cent do not. For the press the figures are reversed, 30 per cent for the former and 56 per cent for the latter.

Work on actual student role performance also has lagged. Knowledge of how students behave in the classroom consists almost wholly of individual psychological matters such as length of attention span, the differences in academic performance of children with different intelligence, the activity levels of boys and girls, and the like. Almost no one has reported on controlled observational studies of what goes on in an educational system between the student(s) and the faculty. One could well ask how the fledgling teacher comes to understand (if he does) the group social processes occurring in his classroom.

What research there is of an orderly nature on the teacher-pupil relation, such as that of Anderson and his colleagues (G-1), already cited, has been focused on other issues, hence provides only a sidelong glance at this problem. The field is thereby open for the introduction of research techniques and theoretical concepts developed by sociology in its study of small groups (G-14). If one were to obtain tape recordings of the interaction in twenty-five third- and twenty-five sixth-grade classrooms, even this type of rudimentary descriptive data currently would be of value. Operating on data like these, or on direct observational data, a series of questions could be asked. What are the relations of role differentiation, phases in group task performance, distribution of participation, variations in types of interactive behavior, and distribution of communication channels to antecedent conditions such as group size, age of members, heterogeneity of sex and intelligence, on the one hand, and to subsequent effects such as the degree of learning, on the other? All these questions can be asked of, and answered by, observational data of the student role with his teacher.

We know that prescriptions for the child in the classroom have varied from one era to another, depending on the theories of child behavior in fashion at the time. Earlier prescriptions were made with little understanding of children's motivation, emotional maturation, and the like. Nowadays prescriptions are tailored to an understanding of these psychological principles. It seems not too much to anticipate an equivalent revolution in thinking resulting from studies in the small group tradition of the interaction patterns in the classroom which, in turn, would indicate some new kinds of classroom organization designed to achieve the aims of the institution.

### Roles with Peers

The second salient aspect of the student's role in the educational system is his relation to his peer group. The research on student-to-student relations consists of two kinds. The first seeks to describe the learning environment outside the classroom from which the student acquires an important part of his education. All schools have their distinctive student cultures, complete with values, status structure, role prescriptions, socialization of new members, and the rest. In new schools the students, lacking such a culture, often take it upon themselves to create one deliberately as in the case of the United States Air Force Academy where the task of the first class was to determine what the "traditions" were to be. Indeed, such new school situations are natural laboratories for the study of the formation of group norms.

One premise of the studies of student culture is that the socializing effect of participation in such a culture is very great (e.g., G-25) and is a less well-recognized but perhaps more important influence on the student's character than is the formal instruction in the classroom. Hence, descriptions of the different social climates of educational institutions and of the student roles therein help to predict the informal learning by the student.

At the secondary school level Hollingshead's work is a recognized classic (G-17) describing the differentiation of student culture along social class lines. The recent intensive study by Wayne Gordon (G-11), to which we refer in more detail later, deals with a single high school and provides further insight into the characteristic student culture. The current study already mentioned under the direction of James Coleman at Chicago makes a comparative study of social climates in two high schools, emphasizing the differences in the activities which give one status and approval in the two schools.

At the higher education level somewhat more interest has been shown. A number of studies (e.g., G-10) of experiences of foreign students in American colleges and universities have been carried out. The most recent contributions are the series of reports sponsored by the Social Science Research Council (G-24). These studies provide many sharp and provocative observations of American college life as one considers how the college environment appears to the foreign student. The work of Kelley (G-18) and the preliminary data (G-26) from the Cornell study already mentioned are important sources. A volume comprising a series of studies from Yale will appear shortly (G-29), and in preparation are major reports from longitudinal studies of college life at Princeton, under the direction of Fred Stephan, and at Vassar under the direction of Nevitt Sanford (G-23).

The second kind of research on the role of the student with other students has looked at what might be termed the interpersonal attractions among students. It frequently has used sociometric measures as its major research tool. The investigations of this kind are impressive in volume if not yet in significant results, and some of the findings may be mentioned by way of exemplification. Happily there are a number of good surveys of this field. Dahlke and Monahan (G-8) have reviewed pertinent materials appearing up to 1949, while the comprehensive review by Lindzey and Borgatta (G-19) includes more recent references, as well as giving the necessary theoretical overview and data on reliability and validity of the sociometric method itself.

The research on interpersonal attraction (G-5, G-15, G-17, G-25) has described the correlates of sociometric choice, pointing out that cliques and informal groups in the school system develop along the lines of social class structure in the community, ecological structure (for example, neighborhood), interest in given types of recreation and in maintaining equivalent academic standing. The research (G-3, G-12) on elementary and secondary schools also has shown that teachers' judgments regarding student relations in their classroom have in general quite low validity, although there is considerable variability among the teachers; that teachers seem unable to locate the isolated (underchosen) individual; and that teachers overestimate the choice-status of children they like and underestimate that of children they dislike.

How have these data and techniques been used? Surprisingly, they have only rarely been pressed into service to the end of enhancing the student's academic learning, but instead are employed to increase the student's adjustment and social acceptability to his peers. It appears (although from informal evidence only) that the aims of the educational system, especially the elementary school, now include the production of "good" social adjustment of the student to his peers. From whatever source this new aim comes, the educators, the students, the public, or all three, it is important to recognize the value of sociometric devices as diagnostic measures of certain aspects of student interaction which teachers fail to perceive accurately, but of which they must be cognizant in order to further this institutional aim of group acceptance.

## Interrelations of Classroom and Peer Group Roles

A third significant issue in the analysis of student roles concerns the interaction effects between the teacher-student and student-student relations. While this issue with respect to educators, that is, the effect of a teacher's relations with his colleagues upon his classroom performance, has apparently not been studied, the situation with respect to students is somewhat better. Taba, in several studies (G-27, G-28), has analyzed the characteristic group life in a number of schools, showing that the peer group climate is a powerful factor in determining not only the values the student learns outside the classroom, but also how he learns in the actual classroom situation. In a recent work in this area, Wayne Gordon (G-11) has described three aspects of a high school culture and developed the major theme that the basic motivating factor of the high school student is to achieve a satisfactory social position within the organization of the school, and specifically within his peer group. Moreover, his behavior both with other students and with the educational personnel in the formal aspects of the institution are best predicted from knowledge of his position within the informal student social system.

A tradition of research on the gifted child, notably expressed in the volume edited by Witty (G-30) in the most recent Yearbook of the National Society for the Study of Education (G-21), and in the recent book by DeHaan and Havighurst (G-9), has shown how desire for peer acceptance where the peer group norms do not favor academic excellence causes the able student to throttle down, so to speak, so as not to outdistance his friends; hence, to protect himself from their ridicule and ostracism. Materials in the forthcoming group of studies on talent development (G-2) will further exemplify the point that peer group norms enhance or detract from the classroom learning, depending on their nature.

In general, all of the work on student roles which describes the student culture, or which analyzes sociometric relations, is of value both in its own right as it describes the environment in which nonacademic matters are learned, and as it is instrumental to achieving the aims of improved social adjustment. This work, however, does not realize its full power until its implications for classroom learning are systematically explored. One of the most thoughtful and influential considerations of the use of pupil norms, culture, and feelings in the educational process is presented by Cantor (G-4). He explores what the teacher can and/or should endeavor to do in drawing the student culture into the educational process. The work includes some provocative transcripts of discussions between teachers of this question, and is well worth the attention of the sociologist.

Ideally, future research on interstudent relations will include as a matter of course the study of the effects of such relations on academic performance. Indeed, there exists the challenging possibility of experimentation in changing student relations, exploring the ways in which various types of student culture and interpersonal relations can be altered so as to expedite learning.

Only a few studies have been concerned with the companion process of the influence of teacher-student relations upon student-student relations. The work by Anderson and his group (G-1) already described in the section on teacher's roles dramatically demonstrates the effect of student-teacher interaction upon the student's behavior toward his peers. Another study (G-6) points to the fact that an authoritarian teacher-pupil relationship seems to interfere with the development of a sociometric structure in the student group, to keep their interpersonal relations formless and in doubt. One question in this area has been raised in so many quarters that it deserves research attention. The question is whether the educators' increasing emphasis upon the student's adjustment to peers has not operated to reduce the student's concern over his relation to the teacher and also to transform this concern so that the student now seeks primarily to demonstrate to the teacher his skills in interpersonal relations rather than his skills in academic pursuits.

### The Student Role in the Community

This topic is included to round out the picture although no one seems to have studied it. One's own observations will readily indicate that the status of student is associated with certain expectations of behavior in the larger community, and with certain kinds of responses of community members. The college student from the small rural village who is honored by his neighbors and the bitter town-gown rivalries in some private university towns are contrasting instances. The misdemeanors of college students are written off as college pranks, even though separated by only a thin line, if at all, from the delinquent acts of the nonstudent youth. Other examples can be adduced of the fact that general student status, as well as the specific type of school (e.g., private) and one's position in it (e.g., football captain), carries with it certain roles in the community.

# VIII

# THE FUNCTIONS OF EDUCATION

CONSIDERATION of the actual functions of education brings one to the end of the institutional analysis. The research of a sociological nature on the functions of education has dealt with several questions. First, research has related the characteristics of institutional processes, such as personnel recruitment, to amount of learning and other changes in the student. Second, research has been concerned with the effect upon learning, occupational performance, and other matters of different educational systems considered as wholes; for example, comparisons of the functions of progressive and traditional schools. Third, there is an important body of research comparing the effects of differing amounts of education, not upon the amount of learning, which would seem naive, but upon other variables such as income and prejudice. These three different interests may be considered in order.

## Variations in Institutional Components

The research of the first type, on the effects of variations in institutional components such as role prescriptions or type of personnel, has been reviewed in the preceding sections pertaining to each component. Examples are the effects upon learning of autocratic versus democratic teacher role performance, and the effects of peer group roles upon academic performance. Evaluation research employing sociological concepts is not extensive. Research of this type has lagged because of the as yet undeveloped appraisal of education in sociological terms. A wide range of possible research studies relating gain in intellectual skills and other personal changes to variations in all of the institutional elements considered in this review awaits the systematic conceptualization of such variations within a broad sociological framework; that is, something other than the traditional description of teaching methods in psychological terms.

In part, too, studies here are difficult because of the problem of adequately controlling for variables not under study and the problem of selecting suitable criterion measures of effect. Since sociology faces these problems along with other disciplines concerned with education, perhaps a further word might be said.

The complexity of a given educational system demands the researcher's attention to the control of variations in aims, resources, personnel characteristics, and the rest, any one of which may operate to produce spurious findings in an evaluation study. The measures of gains in knowledge have progressively improved through the years as better standardized tests appear. References in the Bibliography to the work of the Educational Testing Service and other organizations indicate the continuing attack on this problem. However, where the educational effects of interest to the researcher are other than gain in factual information, the researcher may find it necessary to develop his own measures.

For example, where something such as critical thinking or problem-solving ability is to be appraised, the problem is difficult because of the inadequacy of any current criteria. In spite of the very great desire on the part of both the public and the educational personnel that education train one in the improvement of judgment and thinking, there is as yet no really acceptable measure of this characteristic; and, one might add, we do not actually know in this instance whether participation in the educational institution produces judgment superior to that gained from participation in life outside the school itself.

### Different Types of Educational Systems

A second concern of evaluation studies has been to compare the effects of different educational systems upon behavior in subsequent years. There have been several major investigations of this type. Outstanding is the eight-year follow-up study (H-2) of students from thirty selected experimental (progressive) schools, which report on their college performance. This carefully executed evaluation study, utilizing a matched comparison group from traditional schools, shows that the experimental school graduates in college received better grades and more academic honors, and were more often judged to be systematic and objective in their thinking, to have a high degree of intellectual curiosity and drive, and to be more resourceful in meeting situations. At the same time, they had more nonacademic honors bestowed on them and did not differ from the comparison group in adjustment to their peers.

At the college, in contrast to the secondary school, level the volumes by Knapp and his colleagues (H-8, H-9) show a differential productivity of eminent scientists by different types of undergraduate colleges, suggesting that the educational experience in such colleges develops in the students a higher level of intellectual functioning. The recent report by Holland (E-9), to which we have referred earlier, indicates, however, that the seeming differential productivity is not wholly attributable to characteristics of the schools, but rather involves a differential selectivity of abler students in the first instance. This illustrates the point made before: that the evaluation of the functions of institutions is extremely difficult and requires careful attention to the control of variables such as selection of personnel.

A related study is the well-known report on subscribers to *Time* magazine (H-5), which is truly a mine of information on the correlates of education. However, this study is weakened throughout by inability to control initial selectivity. For example, where it presents data on the differential earning power of persons by field of specialization in college, the rank order by differential earning power is correlated closely with the rank order of intelligence of undergraduate majors in this field as reported by Wolfle (D-21). This indicates again that absence of controls over initial selectivity produces results hard to interpret.

### Different Amounts of Education

A third outstanding type of functional evaluation has sought to describe the effects of differing amounts of education, asking in essence what results accrue to the individual from having been educated.

One of the primary functions of the educational institution apart from transmitting knowledge is alleged to be that of increasing the upward social mobility of the student. The data on this issue are of two types. The first consists of the results found in the literature on social stratification, showing a correlation, which is always large and positive, between amount of education and other class characteristics such as occupational prestige and income. The second consists of direct assessment of such matters as the differential earning power associated with possession of a college education (e.g., H-4). Unfortunately, both the social class data and those from direct assessment studies suffer because of failure to control the initial social class origins of the students, and perhaps more importantly, their intelligence. This permits the argument that any differences which occur are attributable not to education, but to differential selectivity into higher educational levels.

The recent controlled study by Wolfle and Smith (H-15) is therefore of unusual interest. This is a follow-up study of superior high school graduates twenty years after graduation. A comparison of the current incomes of those who attended college and those who had not, equating the two groups on high school rank and intelligence, shows that those who graduated from college were earning from $1,100 to $2,500 more a year than those whose education ended with high school. Increments in income were also associated with high school rank and with intelligence independently of college graduation, but these increments were smaller than those associated with graduation from college.

Anderson (H-1) has attacked this problem somewhat differently, using a sample from the southern states. He notes the traditional relation of education and income, but shows that there is a differential increase, depending on the cultural background of the student. Thus, for whites, the increment in income with increased education tends to be two or three times as large as for nonwhites. A regional comparison shows that education produces greater income increment in the South relative to other parts of the country. Anderson argues that the low income associated with low levels of schooling is less marked outside the

South than within it, and that while the educated person in the South does not get more absolute income than his educated northern counterpart, he gains more because his initial income level is lower.

Another important group of studies has dealt with the effects of education on prejudice. Rose (H-12) has reviewed much of the research on the effects of specific courses; six studies show gains in the reduction of prejudice, four no changes, and one indefinite. Noteworthy reports of work in this area are given by Cook and Cook (H-3), and by Taba, Brady, and Robinson (H-14). The latter describes four years of experimental work on intergroup education in some nineteen school systems in different states and indicates the success of such programs in the improvement in democratic relations.

Studies of the effects of the amount of education on prejudice have been reviewed in Brookover (A-1: pp. 130–132), and more recently an important study of the relation of education and discriminatory attitudes in southern whites has been presented (H-6). All these studies show that prejudice is inversely related to educational attainment. Again, in most of these, control of other variables such as differential selection of students is lacking.

A third group of studies of educational effects considers the influence of college attendance upon student personality. One of the largest interests has been in the effects of college upon the values of the students. During the past generation and more perhaps several hundred studies of changes in college student values have been made. In a very important book (H-7) Jacob has summarized the studies dealing with the effects of curricular matters upon student values. One general fact which emerges is that there is more homogeneity in values of college students at the end of their college experience than at the beginning. As Jacob puts it, the effect of college is not so much to liberalize as it is to socialize the individual into the ranks of college alumni. A second fact discovered by this body of research is that while there are some studies which show value changes, the great majority of studies indicate that the influence of college courses upon the student values is negligible. Specific studies of variations in the curriculum involving comparisons of general education programs, liberal arts programs, professional versus vocational courses, experimental courses, and social science courses, show no discernible changes in student values related to one or another of these programs. Other studies have been specifically concerned with the influence of different instructors—for example, those rated "good" or "bad" by students, or liked or disliked, and with variations in teaching methods; like the studies of the curriculum, these, too, show no value changes attributable to such variations in educational procedure. The research shows that certain types of colleges, considered as wholes, may have a distinctive effect upon the students' values. These tend to be private colleges with small enrollments, such as Antioch and Bennington, and here, of course, one must raise again the question of error introduced through failure to control initial selection of students. Certainly Bennington, for instance, draws a highly distinctive student body. All of this research, then, points to the conclusion that the curriculum in college influences one's knowledge rather than one's values, and suggests rather strongly that what value changes do occur in students may be more closely related to their participation in the college student culture than in the classroom.

The study by Newcomb (H-11) describes changes in the liberality of student attitudes from freshman to senior year and shows clearly that it is the peer reference group of the student which primarily determines the shift in attitudes. The continuing study of Vassar students mentioned before has produced a first report (H-13). The initial findings show that seniors, in contrast to freshmen, differ significantly in several ways: they are lower in authoritarianism, conventionality, passivity, and in feminine sensitivity; they are higher in flexibility, tolerance of ambiguity, freedom from compulsiveness, and a number of other variables which indicate a general lessening of repression. Reference was made earlier in the chapter on student roles to the study of the Princeton undergraduate which has been under way for several years and has focused on similar matters.

The growth of interest in research of this type has lead to the recent establishment of the Social Science Research Council's

Committee on Personality Development in Youth. This committee will develop plans for advancing research on the social, personal, and intellectual development of individuals of college age in social environments of different kinds. Ralph Tyler is the current chairman of the committee.

Much research remains to be done on other functions of American education. For twelve to sixteen years after the age of six a good share of a person's life is spent in the educational environment. Along with the home the school provides the primary learning experiences of the individual, and our current society reflects in countless ways the experiences one has had in this environment. Why not inquire, therefore, into the effects on sex-role learning of participation in schools segregated by sex in contrast to coeducational schools? Or into the value of the rating and dating experience during high school and college for later life marital success? Note the fact that the proportion of females to males among teachers is much greater at the lower levels. What are the implications of this, recognizing that the elementary school environment is present during the latency phase of child development, and the secondary school environment during the adolescent period. Mead (H-10) has argued that the allocation of female teachers to the elementary grades, but males to the secondary schools, is just not whimsy but has its roots deep in the primitive past, suggesting some hidden but fundamental rationale. As a last query, how may social grouping in the school, for example, homogeneous ability classes, high school sororities and fraternities, differentially bring about the development of a democratic attitude among the students?

For the sociologist to view the institution of education as a major cultural learning experience for all individuals in our society, and to take a hard look at some of the hidden functions of this experience, particularly those aspects of it that occur outside the classroom and without reference to the avowed aims of the institution, must provide a major insight into the sources of the American spirit and the adult social structure.

# THE ROLES OF THE SOCIOLOGIST IN EDUCATIONAL TRAINING AND RESEARCH

IN THIS FINAL SECTION we consider the ways in which existing resources of sociology are brought to the attention of educators, and the capacities in which sociologists have ordinarily carried on their research on education. Ways in which these teaching and research functions might be extended are then explored.

### The Current Situation

Almost all educational personnel during their training for teaching or administration at the elementary and secondary school levels take courses in sociology. At present the two major functions of this training are to provide content for subsequent teaching and to provide insight into the sociological aspects of education, that is, such matters as have been considered in this review. With respect to the first of these, even though there is no specially designated content area of sociology below the college level, the social studies teachers have frequently majored in sociology in schools of education, or have had sociology required as part of their specialization in this area. With respect to the second, the aim is to have the educator bring to his role a broader understanding of the basic social processes of the educational system.

The way in which sociological training of either type is provided varies from one institution to another. At least four patterns can be discerned. In what is probably their rank order of frequency, they are as follows: (1) Students are sent from schools of education into departments of sociology for courses in sociology. This pattern is followed at the Universities of Wisconsin and

Michigan, for example. (2) Sociologists are on the staff of a school of education or a teacher training institution. Examples here are the University of California (Berkeley) and Teachers College of Columbia University. (3) Schools of education maintain their own distinct department of sociology staffed by sociologists. New York University is an example of this pattern. Last, one finds the pattern in which the interests of sociology and education are joined through interdisciplinary committees or similar groups representing separate departments or schools. The Committee on Human Development at the University of Chicago is a case in point.

The second aspect of the role of the sociologist concerns the capacity in which he has carried on his research on education. Positions now range from those completely external to any school or department of education, such as the ordinary role of the sociologist in his own academic department, to positions of central responsibility, such as Wilbur Brookover's directorship of the Bureau of Educational Research at Michigan State University.

There is no clear relation between the position of the sociologist and the type or amount of research done as a whole. Thus, the work of Lazarsfeld and Thielens, of Gross, of Charters, and of Havighurst is associated with varying roles with respect to educational groups. It would appear, however, that though the bulk of research has been carried out by sociologists not directly involved in departments or schools of education, the per capita rate of educational research is considerably greater for the sociologists holding positions in part in education, usually of the combined type described above. To be sure, in the latter case the research may be part of the formal duties associated with such positions, but the easier access to research sites and subjects, that is, school systems themselves, is an important factor.

There are some disadvantages in each of the current patterns which have worked against the greater development of the sociological study of education. Where the sociologist has only a regular appointment in his own department, and deals with education at a distance, so to speak, in his teaching and research, the teaching materials often are not adequately adapted to the interests of educators, and the research usually consists of discrete and isolated studies, which do not build upon the work which has been done before and which are not developed further by the sociologist in his subsequent career.

Where the sociologist has an appointment in, or is otherwise directly involved with, an educational school or department, the disadvantages, three in number, are of a different kind. The first pertains to the career of the sociologist and must be dealt with quite frankly. It has not been prestigeful for sociologists to hold positions in schools of education, in spite of the outstanding sociologists who have held and who currently hold such positions. Considerations mentioned in the introduction—the probability of being confused with nonsociologists who teach the same subject matter, the fact that education has lower prestige than, say, medicine or law, hence being connected with education has less prestige than working on a medical or law faculty, the fact that until recently sociology has moved away from applied interests— all are factors which must be faced realistically. Thus, the sociologist's research is received with less interest than is research in other areas; he himself may find it awkward to explain his professional position, and the image of himself he receives from other sociologists may raise some nagging doubts as to whether he should be content to study education.

It must be stressed that the educator himself does not look down upon the sociologist, but on the contrary is acquainted with the type of contribution he can make and with its importance and holds it in high value. This results in a comparatively happy working relationship between sociologist and educator. Indeed, one might add that the educators have been too accepting and too uncritical, if anything. This situation contrasts with that where the sociologist works with the physician, the lawyer, or the psychiatrist where the initial doubt, resistance, even rejection is considerably greater.

A second disadvantage is that the sociologist often becomes isolated from his fellows, and thus is increasingly drawn into the field of education, leaving his sociology behind. Without the continuing invigoration of contact with other sociologists on a professional basis, his courses and his research become centered on the problems of education rather than the contributions of sociology, and what sociology remains is soon dated.

This observation is made in spite of certain studies suggesting the contrary. Herrington (I-4) has reported a decline over the years in applied or "educational sociology" courses and an increase in the number of general ("pure") courses given in teachers' colleges and schools of education. Another study supports this. Landis (I-5), in his review of more than 1,000 courses in sociology offered in 162 teachers' colleges, finds they are organized around the traditional subdivisions of sociology rather than applied topics.

The fact is that much of what passes under the name of sociological training of educators is carried on by persons trained in education, not sociology. One must recognize that unfortunately the materials presented are frequently pseudosociology, consisting of moralistic and philosophical content rather than research and theory. They may be variously termed, such as social stratification, community organization, or the family, but they often turn out to be sociology in name only.

A third disadvantage is that the sociologist in this role lacks graduate students in sociology with whom he can work. For many this takes from them one of the deepest satisfactions of the career of teaching, participation in the training of a new generation of scientists. Often the frustration causes the sociologist to seek to make research social scientists out of the students in education whom he does teach. This strikes one as an understandable but misguided effort, with probable loss to both sociology and education. It is not, of course, that education students should not become sociologists if they wish, but that just as soon as they do they are no longer practicing educators and are lost to their own profession. It is unrealistic to ask the practicing educator to carry on his own basic research and to train him to do so. Much more fruitful is training which sensitizes him to the need for research, which makes him critical of unfounded generalizations about social behavior and which equips him to participate during his career on research projects with social scientists, both to his own benefit as Corey has so convincingly argued (I-2), and to theirs.

## Some Directions for the Future

The actual participation of sociologists as members of the faculty of schools of education, and the provision of courses organized so that they are neither esoteric sociology nor traditional "educational sociology" but instead relate the two fields to the enrichment of both has advantages not found in other arrangements. The problem, as indicated above, is that the sociologist must continuously strive to maintain his professional identity.

A solution to this specific problem has been increasingly in evidence in recent years, consisting of the simple step of establishing joint appointments in sociology and education. At Harvard, Chicago, the University of California, Michigan State University, to name but a few, this pattern is followed with success. The merits of this arrangement will be clear. The sociologist stays a sociologist first, and a student of education second; his research and teaching in education is constantly refreshed through contact with his colleagues and performance of his duties in his own department of sociology.

There is a further advantage in this dual role of the sociologist, namely, the graduate student in sociology can join him in the study of education as a legitimate enterprise, with the result that new specialists in the area are produced. Without this arrangement, the graduate student with an interest in the sociology of education has much greater difficulty in obtaining the auspices of both sociologists and educators which he needs to carry out his research. This is not a minor matter. At present there are very few locations where the graduate student in sociology can receive systematic training in research on education, and because of the recent resurgence of interest there is actually a shortage of trained personnel.

Where this is not done, but where sociologists have traditional appointments, their studies of education should be strengthened through greater effort on their part to relate their work to other research in the field. We have mentioned the failure to do this in many instances under current conditions. The fact that the sociological study of education has not been a clearly defined area of inquiry accounts for it in part. A second contributing factor is that many sociologists have quite rightly viewed the field of education as an arena for testing their hypotheses, but have stressed the implications of the research for the sociological problem to which the hypothesis pertains and not for education. One needs only to recognize the twofold contribution of any sociological research on education, one to sociologists and the other to educators, to see that this situation can be improved through the attention of the researcher to the further implications of his study for the practice of education.

It is true that the opportunities for research on education may be more difficult to develop in this role than is the case where the sociologist is directly connected with schools or colleges of education. The latter will have easier access to subjects and locale, and usually more enthusiastic cooperation from educators throughout the course of the research. This is not true, however, with respect to institutions of higher learning, which leads us to consideration of one of the cardinal values of the study of education. For the sociologist who lacks the customary opportunities for research, he should find that his own academic institution provides problems and data which are highly accessible and of utmost importance, and that research on his own environment is as good a place as any to begin. Indeed, the university is an example *par excellence* of the type of social organization which sociologists are especially equipped to study. Almost all of the research questions raised in the preceding pages, for example, student culture, colleague interaction, recruitment of faculty, and the like, pertain to the college or university, and their answers lie close to one's hand.

There is yet a third possible development which deserves our closing comments. We refer to potential roles of sociologists in either a research or consultant capacity in educational systems. It is startling to be unable to find any sociologist who is currently employed on a regular basis in any of the major public school systems in this country. The school system in New York City employs, by way of contrast, more than one hundred psychologists but no sociologists. School systems continually face a series of operating problems, such as when and where to build new schools so as to be congruent both with population demands and community norms, how to recruit and maintain an adequate educational staff, how to deal most constructively with the dissident, not to speak of delinquent, groups in the student body, and many others we have mentioned. These involve aspects of human behavior on which sociologists are acknowledged authorities. One might wish to go on and take the strong position that it is difficult to understand how current school systems can be operated in other than an anachronistic manner without drawing on the modern resources of sociology.

At the university level the same argument applies. From time to time universities have established their own internal research divisions, staffed by competent social scientists. Such existed for a while at the University of Chicago, and does today at Princeton, Vassar, and a few other locations. These have been *ad hoc* units, however, set up to study a specific set of educational questions and terminated after a period of time. It remains, then, a stimulating prospect for the future that universities may utilize sociologists in the continuing and systematic study of their own operations.

We have indicated several types of roles which the sociologist might wish to take in the study of education. In the hope that sociologists will be attracted in greater numbers to this field of endeavor, we might recapitulate just three points: research funds are available; educators are willing, even enthusiastic, to give support; some of the most fundamental problems of sociology are manifest in the educational process and await attention. There seems little more that the serious scientist would want.

# SELECTED BIBLIOGRAPHY

# SELECTED BIBLIOGRAPHY

It is EXPECTED that the sociologist interested in education will be acquainted with the work appearing in the regular sociological sources, both books and journals. It is of value also to review the sections on education in *Child Development Abstracts* and *Psychological Abstracts* as the issues are published during the year.

In addition to these customary sources, there are several of a specialized nature which have materials pertinent to sociology and education and which might escape the sociologist's attention in the normal course of events. Among regularly issued journals research of interest appears in the *Harvard Educational Review, Journal of Educational Sociology, Journal of Educational Research, Journal of Experimental Education, Review of Educational Research, School and Society,* and *The School Review.*

The *Education Index* presents a monthly listing of significant articles and books in the field of education.

Attention is focused on the field of higher education in the *American Association of University Professors Bulletin* and it carries articles on all aspects of higher educational institutions.

In the area of personnel selection and of evaluation the periodical publication of the Educational Testing Service, *ETS Developments,* and the various publications of the College Entrance Examination Board describing its activities serve to keep one informed of current developments.

The National Educational Association, the major professional organization of elementary and secondary school educators, carries on through its numerous affiliates and standing committees a broad program of research and publication. The sociologist should be familiar with the most recent comprehensive *Publications List* (1956) available from the central office in Washington, D. C. Last, the Division of State and Local Systems, the Research and Statistical Services Branch, and the Division of Higher Education, all of the Office of Education of the federal government, collect and have available for distribution upon request a wealth of statistical data pertaining to the educational system which provides the descriptive backbone of any comparative study.

In the pages that follow, the sources cited have been grouped accordting to the topics for which they have particular relevance.

A. *General*

1. BROOKOVER, WILBUR B., *A Sociology of Education*. American Book Co., New York, 1955.

2. CONRAD, RICHARD, "A Systematic Analysis of Current Researches in the Sociology of Education," *American Sociological Review*, vol. 17, 1952, pp. 350–355.

3. DAHLKE, H. OTTO, *Values in Culture and Classroom:* A Study of the Sociology of the School. Harper and Bros., New York, 1958.

4. GROSS, NEAL, "Problems and Prospects in the Sociology of Education" in *Current Problems and Prospects in Sociology* (tentative title). Major papers delivered at the 52nd Annual Meeting of the American Sociological Society, 1957, edited by Leonard Broom, Leonard S. Cottrell, Jr., and Robert K. Merton. Basic Books, New York. (In press)

5. HAVIGHURST, ROBERT J., AND BERNICE L. NEUGARTEN, *Society and Education*. Allyn and Bacon, Boston, 1957.

6. MERCER, BLAINE E., AND EDWIN R. CARR, *Education and the Social Order*. Rinehart and Co., New York, 1957.

B. *Aims of Education*

1. BUTTS, N. FREEMAN, *A Cultural History of Western Education*. 2d ed. McGraw-Hill Book Co., New York, 1955.

2. CHARTERS, W. W., JR., "Social Class Analysis and the Control of Public Education," *Harvard Educational Review*, vol. 23, 1953, pp. 268–283.

3. DURKHEIM, EMILE, *Education and Sociology*. The Free Press, Glencoe, Ill., 1956.

4. EDUCATIONAL POLICIES COMMISSION, *The Purposes of Education in American Democracy*. National Education Association, Washington, 1938.

5. FRENCH, WILL, AND ASSOCIATES, *Behavioral Goals of General Education in High School*. Russell Sage Foundation, New York, 1957.

6. GROSS, NEAL, AND ALEXANDER W. McEACHERN, *Who Runs Our Schools?* John Wiley and Sons, New York. (In press)

7. HINES, VYNCE A., AND ROBERT L. CURRAN, "The School and Community Forces," *Review of Educational Research*, vol. 25, 1955, pp. 48–60.

8. JOHNSON, CHARLES S., "Education and the Cultural Process: Introduction to Symposium," *American Journal of Sociology*, vol. 48, 1943, pp. 629–632.

9. KEARNEY, NOLAN C., *Elementary School Objectives*. Russell Sage Foundation, New York, 1953.

10. KREITLOW, BURTON W., "School-Community Relations," *Review of Educational Research*, vol. 25, 1955, pp. 299–318.

11. KREITLOW, BURTON W., AND JAMES A. DUNCAN, *The Acceptance of Educational Programs in Rural Wisconsin*. University of Wisconsin, Bulletin 525, Madison, Wis., 1956.

12. LIEBERMAN, MYRON, *Education as a Profession*. Prentice-Hall, New York, 1956.

13. MULHERN, JAMES, *A History of Education*. Ronald Press Co., New York, 1946.

14. NATIONAL OPINION RESEARCH CENTER, *The Public Looks at Education*. The Center, University of Denver, Report No. 21, Denver, 1944.

15. PRESIDENT'S COMMISSION ON HIGHER EDUCATION, "Establishing the Goals," vol. 1 of *Higher Education for American Democracy*. Government Printing Office, Washington, 1947; and Harper and Bros., New York, 1947.

16. REMMERS, H. H., AND D. H. RADLER, *The American Teenager*. Bobbs-Merrill Co., New York, 1957.

17. ROPER, ELMO, "Higher Education: The Fortune Survey," *Supplement to Fortune*, September, 1949.

18. SLOCUM, WALTER L., *Occupational and Educational Plans of High School Seniors from Farm and Non-Farm Families*. State College of Washington, Institute of Agricultural Sciences, Pullman, Wash., 1956.

19. SPINDLER, GEORGE D., EDITOR, *Education and Anthropology*. Stanford University Press, Stanford, Calif., 1955.

20. SUCHMAN, EDWARD A., "The Values of American College Students" in *Long Range Planning for Education: Report of the 22nd Educational Conference*. American Council on Education, Washington, 1958.

C. *Allocation of Materials*

1. ASHMORE, HARRY S., *The Negro and the Schools.* University of North Carolina Press, Chapel Hill, 1954.

2. LIEBERMAN, MYRON, *Education as a Profession.* Prentice-Hall, New York, 1956.

3. MILLETT, JOHN D., *Financing Higher Education in the United States.* Columbia University Press, New York, 1952.

4. MORT, PAUL R., AND WALTER C. REUSSER, *Public School Finance.* 2d ed. McGraw-Hill Book Co., New York, 1951.

5. RUML, BEARDSLEY, AND SIDNEY G. TICKTON, *Teaching Salaries Then and Now: A 50-Year Comparison with Other Occupations and Industries.* The Fund for the Advancement of Education, Bulletin No. 1, New York, 1955.

6. WARNER, W. LLOYD, ROBERT J. HAVIGHURST, AND MARTIN B. LOEB, *Who Shall Be Educated?* Harper and Bros., New York, 1944.

7. WEST, ELMER D., EDITOR, *Background for a National Scholarship Policy.* American Council on Education, Washington, 1956.

D. *Allocation of Personnel: The Educators*

1. BARR, ARVIL S., DAVID E. EUSTICE, AND EDWARD J. NOE, "The Measurement and Prediction of Teacher Efficiency," *Review of Educational Research,* vol. 25, 1955, pp. 261–269.

2. BECKER, HOWARD S., "The Career of the Chicago Public Schoolteacher," *American Journal of Sociology,* vol. 57, 1952, pp. 470–477.

3. BECKER, HOWARD S., "Schools and Systems of Social Status," *Phylon,* vol. 16, 1955, pp. 159–170.

4. BROOKOVER, WILBUR B., *A Sociology of Education.* American Book Co., New York, 1955.

5. CAPLOW, THEODORE, AND REECE McGEE, *The Academic Marketplace.* Basic Books, New York. (In press)

6. CHARTERS, W. W., JR., "Survival in the Profession: A Criterion for Selecting Teacher Trainees," *Journal of Teacher Education,* vol. 7, 1956, pp. 253–255.

7. GREENHOE, FLORENCE, *Community Contacts and Participation of Teachers*. American Council on Public Affairs, Washington, 1941.

8. HAVIGHURST, ROBERT J., AND BERNICE L. NEUGARTEN, *Society and Education*. Allyn and Bacon, Boston, 1957.

9. HOLLINGSHEAD, AUGUST B., "Climbing the Academic Ladder," *American Sociological Review*, vol. 5, 1940, pp. 384–394.

10. LIEBERMAN, MYRON, *Education as a Profession*. Prentice-Hall, New York, 1956.

11. MASON, WARD S., AND NEAL GROSS, "Intra-occupational Prestige Differentiation: The School Superintendency," *American Sociological Review*, vol. 20, 1955, pp. 326–331.

12. MERCER, BLAINE E., AND EDWIN R. CARR, *Education and the Social Order*. Rinehart and Co., New York, 1957.

13. NATIONAL OPINION RESEARCH CENTER, "Jobs and Occupations: A Popular Evaluation" in *Class, Status and Power: A Reader in Social Stratification*, edited by Reinhard Bendix and Seymour M. Lipset. The Free Press, Glencoe, Ill., 1953, pp. 411–426.

14. RICHEY, ROBERT W., WILLIAM H. FOX, AND CHARLES E. FAUSET, "Prestige Ranks of Teaching," *Occupations*, vol. 30, 1951, pp. 33–35.

15. SIMEON, J. DOMAS, AND DAVID TIEDEMAN, "Teacher Competence: An Annotated Bibliography," *Journal of Experimental Education*, vol. 19, 1950, pp. 101–218.

16. SOROKIN, PITIRIM A., *Society, Culture, and Personality: Their Structure and Dynamics*. Harper and Bros., New York, 1947, pp. 217–420.

17. STILES, LINDLEY J., EDITOR, *The Teacher's Role in American Society*. Harper and Bros., New York, 1957.

18. TERRIEN, FREDERIC W., "The Occupational Roles of Teachers," *Journal of Educational Sociology*, vol. 29, 1955, pp. 14–20.

19. WILSON, LOGAN, *The Academic Man*. Oxford University Press, New York, 1942.

20. WOODBURNE, LLOYD S., *Faculty Personnel Policies in Higher Education*. Harper and Bros., New York, 1950.

21. WOLFLE, DAEL, *America's Resources of Specialized Talent*. Harper and Bros., New York, 1954.

E. *Allocation of Personnel: The Students*

1. ALLEN, CHARLES M., *Combating the Dropout Problem.* Science Research Associates, Chicago, 1956.

2. AMERICAN COUNCIL ON EDUCATION, *On Getting Into College:* A Study Made for the Committee on Discriminations in College Admissions. The Council, Washington, 1949.

3. BALDWIN, ALFRED L., URIE BRONFENBRENNER, DAVID C. McCLELLAND, AND FRED L. STRODTBECK, *Talent and Society.* D. Van Nostrand Co., New York. (In press)

4. BERNERT, ELEANOR H., *America's Children.* John Wiley and Sons, New York, 1958.

5. DAVIS, ALLISON, *Social-Class Influences Upon Learning.* Harvard University Press, Cambridge, Mass., 1948.

6. EELLS, KENNETH, AND OTHERS, *Intelligence and Cultural Differences.* University of Chicago Press, Chicago, 1951.

7. FUND FOR THE ADVANCEMENT OF EDUCATION, *They Went to College Early.* Evaluation Report Number 2. The Fund, New York, 1957.

8. HAVIGHURST, ROBERT J., AND BERNICE L. NEUGARTEN, *Society and Education.* Allyn and Bacon, Boston, 1957.

9. HOLLAND, JOHN L., "Undergraduate Origins of American Scientists," *Science*, vol. 126, no. 3271, 1957, pp. 433-437.

10. HOLLINGSHEAD, AUGUST B., *Elmtown's Youth.* John Wiley and Sons, New York, 1949.

11. HYMAN, HERBERT H., "The Value Systems of Different Classes: A Social Psychological Contribution to the Analyses of Stratification" in *Class, Status and Power: A Reader in Social Stratification*, edited by Reinhard Bendix and Seymour M. Lipset. The Free Press, Glencoe, Ill., 1953, pp. 426-442.

12. KAHL, JOSEPH A., "Educational and Occupational Aspirations of 'Common Man' Boys," *Harvard Educational Review*, vol. 23, 1953, pp. 186-203.

13. McARTHUR, CHARLES, "Personalities of Public and Private School Boys," *Harvard Educational Review*, vol. 24, 1954, pp. 256-262.

14. MULLIGAN, RAYMOND A., "Socioeconomic Background and College Enrollment," *American Sociological Review*, vol. 16, 1951, pp. 188-196.

15. MULLIGAN, RAYMOND A., "Social Characteristics of College Students," *American Sociological Review*, vol. 18, 1953, pp. 305–310.

16. ROSEN, BERNARD C., "The Achievement Syndrome: A Psycho-cultural Dimension of Social Stratification," *American Sociological Review*, vol. 21, 1956, pp. 203–211.

17. SEWELL, WILLIAM H., ARCHIE O. HALLER, AND MURRAY A. STRAUS, "Social Status and Educational and Occupational Aspiration," *American Sociological Review*, vol. 22, 1957, pp. 67–73.

18. SIBLEY, ELBRIDGE, "Some Demographic Clues to Stratification," *American Sociological Review*, vol. 7, 1942, pp. 322–330.

19. SUCHMAN, EDWARD A., JOHN P. DEAN, ROBIN M. WILLIAMS, AND OTHERS, *Desegregation:* Some Propositions and Research Suggestions. Anti-Defamation League of B'nai B'rith, New York, 1958.

20. TERMAN, LEWIS M., AND MELITA H. ODEN, *The Gifted Child Grows Up:* Twenty-five Years' Follow-up of a Superior Group. Stanford University Press, Stanford, Calif., 1947.

21. WILLIAMS, ROBIN M., AND MARGARET W. RYAN, EDITORS, *Schools in Transition.* University of North Carolina Press, Chapel Hill, 1954.

F. **The Roles of the Educator**

1. ANDERSON, HAROLD H., AND COLLABORATORS, *Studies of Teachers' Classroom Personalities.* Parts I, II, III. Applied Psychology Monographs of the American Psychological Association, Stanford University Press, Stanford, Calif., 1945–1946.

2. BECKER, HOWARD S., "Social-Class Variations in the Teacher-Pupil Relationship," *Journal of Educational Sociology*, vol. 25, 1952.

3. BECKER, HOWARD S., AND JAMES W. CARPER, "The Development of Identification with an Occupation," *American Journal of Sociology*, vol. 61, 1956, pp. 289–298.

4. BROOKOVER, WILBUR B., "The Social Roles of Teachers and Pupil Achievement," *American Sociological Review*, vol. 8, 1943, pp. 389–393.

F.   *The Roles of the Educator—Continued*

5. BROOKOVER, WILBUR B., "The Relation of Social Factors to Teaching Ability," *Journal of Experimental Education,* vol. 13, 1945, pp. 191–205.

6. BROOKOVER, WILBUR B., *A Sociology of Education.* American Book Co., New York, 1955.

7. BRUBACHER, JOHN S., *History of the Problems of Education.* McGraw-Hill Book Co., New York, 1947.

8. BUSH, ROBERT N., *The Teacher-Pupil Relationship.* Prentice-Hall, New York, 1954.

9. CRONBACH, LEE J., *Educational Psychology.* Harcourt, Brace and Co., New York, 1954.

10. GETZELS, J. W., AND EGON G. GUBA, "The Structure of Roles and Role Conflict in the Teaching Situation," *Journal of Educational Sociology,* vol. 29, 1955, pp. 30–40.

11. GREENHOE, FLORENCE, *Community Contacts and Participation of Teachers.* American Council on Public Affairs, Washington, 1941.

12. GRONLUND, NORMAN E., "Relationship Between the Sociometric Status of Pupils and Teachers' Preferences For or Against Having Them in Class," *Sociometry,* vol. 16, 1953, pp. 142–150.

13. GROSS, NEAL, "A Critique of 'Social Class Structure and American Education,' " *Harvard Educational Review,* vol. 23, 1953, pp. 298–329.

14. GROSS, NEAL, *The Schools and the Press.* New England School Development Council, Cambridge, Mass., 1956.

15. GROSS, NEAL C., WARD S. MASON, AND ALEXANDER W. MCEACHERN, *Explorations in Role Analysis:* Studies of the School Superintendency Role. John Wiley and Sons, New York, 1958.

16. GROSS, NEAL, AND ALEXANDER W. MCEACHERN, *Who Runs Our Schools?* John Wiley and Sons, New York. (In press)

17. HINES, VYNCE A., AND ROBERT L. CURRAN, "The School and Community Forces," *Review of Educational Research,* vol. 25, 1955, pp. 48–60.

18. HOLLINGSHEAD, AUGUST B., *Elmtown's Youth.* John Wiley and Sons, New York, 1949.

19. JENKINS, DAVID H., AND RONALD LIPPITT, *Interpersonal Perceptions of Teachers, Students, and Parents.* National Education Association, Division of Adult Education Service, Washington, 1951.

20. KREITLOW, BURTON W., "School-Community Relations," *Review of Educational Research,* vol. 25, 1955, pp. 299–318.

21. LAZARSFELD, PAUL, AND WAGNER THIELENS, *The Academic Mind:* Social Scientists in a Time of Crisis. The Free Press, Glencoe, Ill. (In press)

22. REMMERS, H. H., AND D. H. RADLER, *The American Teenager.* Bobbs-Merrill Co., New York, 1957.

23. RICHEY, ROBERT W., AND WILLIAM H. FOX, *An Analysis of Various Factors Associated with the Selection of Teaching as a Vocation.* Bulletin of the School of Education, Division of Research and Field Services, Indiana University, Bloomington, Ind., May, 1948.

24. RILEY, JOHN W., JR., BRYCE F. RYAN, AND MARCIA LIFSHITZ, *The Student Looks at His Teacher.* Rutgers University Press, New Brunswick, N. J., 1950.

25. SEEMAN, MELVIN, "Role Conflict and Ambivalence in Leadership," *American Sociological Review,* vol. 18, 1953, pp. 373–380.

26. SMITH, B. OTHANEL, WILLIAM O. STANLEY, AND J. HARLAN SHORES, *Fundamentals of Curriculum Development.* World Book Co., Yonkers, N. Y., 1950.

27. STILES, LINDLEY J., EDITOR, *The Teacher's Role in American Society.* Harper and Bros., 1957.

28. SUCHMAN, EDWARD A., "The Values of American College Students" in *Long Range Planning for Education:* Report of the 22nd Educational Conference. American Council on Education, Washington, 1958.

29. TERRIEN, FREDERIC W., "Who Thinks What About Educators?" *American Journal of Sociology,* vol. 59, 1953, pp. 150–158.

30. TERRIEN, FREDERIC W., "The Occupational Roles of Teachers," *Journal of Educational Sociology,* vol. 29, 1955, pp. 14–20.

31. WALLER, WILLARD, *The Sociology of Teaching.* John Wiley and Sons, New York, 1932.

32. WILSON, LOGAN, *The Academic Man.* Oxford University Press, New York, 1942.

G. *The Roles of the Student*

1. ANDERSON, HAROLD H., AND COLLABORATORS, *Studies of Teachers' Classroom Personalities.* Parts I, II, III. Applied Psychology Monographs of the American Psychological Association, Stanford University Press, Stanford, Calif., 1945–1946.

2. BALDWIN, ALFRED L., URIE BRONFENBRENNER, DAVID C. McCLELLAND, AND FRED L. STRODTBECK, *Talent and Society.* D. Van Nostrand Co., New York. (In press)

3. BONNEY, MERL E., "Sociometric Study of Agreement Between Teacher Judgments and Student Choices: In Regard to the Number of Friends Possessed by High School Students," *Sociometry,* vol. 10, 1947, pp. 133–146.

4. CANTOR, NATHANIEL, *The Teaching ⟷ Learning Process.* Dryden Press, New York, 1953.

5. COOK, LLOYD A., "An Experimental Sociographic Study of a Stratified 10th Grade Class," *American Sociological Review,* vol. 10, 1945, pp. 250–261.

6. CUNNINGHAM, RUTH, AND ASSOCIATES, *Understanding Group Behavior of Boys and Girls.* Bureau of Publications, Teachers College, Columbia University, New York, 1951.

7. DAHLKE, H. OTTO, *Values in Culture and Classroom: A Study in the Sociology of the School.* Harper and Bros., New York, 1958.

8. DAHLKE, H. OTTO, AND THOMAS O. MONAHAN, "Problems in the Application of Sociometry to Schools," *The School Review,* vol. 57, 1949, pp. 223–234.

9. DeHAAN, ROBERT F., AND ROBERT J. HAVIGHURST, *Educating Gifted Children.* University of Chicago Press, Chicago, 1957.

10. DuBOIS, CORA, *Foreign Students and Higher Education in the United States.* American Council on Education, Washington, 1956.

11. GORDON, C. WAYNE, *The Social System of the High School: A Study in the Sociology of Adolescence.* The Free Press, Glencoe, Ill., 1957.

12. GRONLUND, NORMAN E., "The Accuracy of Teachers' Judgments Concerning the Sociometric Status of Sixth-Grade Pupils," *Sociometry,* vol. 13, 1950, part 1, pp. 197–225; part 2, pp. 329–357.

13. GROSS, NEAL, *The Schools and the Press*. New England School Development Council, Cambridge, Mass., 1956.

14. HARE, PAUL, EDGAR F. BORGATTA, AND ROBERT F. BALES, EDITORS, *Small Groups:* Studies in Social Interaction. Alfred A. Knopf, New York, 1955.

15. HAVIGHURST, ROBERT J., AND BERNICE L. NEUGARTEN, *Society and Education*. Allyn and Bacon, Boston, 1957.

16. HENRY, JULES, "Attitude Organization in Elementary School Classrooms," *American Journal of Orthopsychiatry*, vol. 27, 1957, pp. 117–133.

17. HOLLINGSHEAD, AUGUST B., *Elmtown's Youth*. John Wiley and Sons, New York, 1949.

18. KELLEY, JANET A., *College Life and the Mores*. Bureau of Publications, Teachers College, Columbia University, New York, 1949.

19. LINDZEY, GARDNER, AND EDGAR F. BORGATTA, "Sociometric Measurement" in *Handbook of Social Psychology*, edited by Gardner Lindzey. Addison Wesley Press, Cambridge, Mass., 1954, vol. 1, chap. 2.

20. MITCHELL, J. C., "A Study of Teachers' and Mental Hygienists' Ratings of Certain Behavior Problems of Children," *Journal of Educational Research*, vol. 36, 1943, pp. 292–307.

21. NATIONAL SOCIETY FOR THE STUDY OF EDUCATION, *Education for the Gifted:* 57th Yearbook, Part II. University of Chicago Press (distributor), Chicago, 1958.

22. REMMERS, H. H., AND D. H. RADLER, *The American Teenager*. Bobbs-Merrill Co., New York, 1957.

23. SANFORD, NEVITT (ISSUE EDITOR), "Personality Development During the College Years," *The Journal of Social Issues*, vol. 12, no. 4, 1956, pp. 1–70.

24. SMITH, M. BREWSTER (ISSUE EDITOR), "Attitudes and Adjustment in Cross-Cultural Contact: Recent Studies of Foreign Students," *The Journal of Social Issues*, vol. 12, no. 1, 1956, pp. 1–70.

25. SMUCKER, ORDEN, "The Campus Clique as an Agency of Socialization," *Journal of Educational Sociology*, vol. 21, 1947, pp. 163–168.

G. *The Roles of the Student—Continued*

26. SUCHMAN, EDWARD A., "The Values of American College Students" in *Long Range Planning for Education:* Report of the 22nd Educational Conference. American Council on Education, Washington, 1958.

27. TABA, HILDA, *School Culture:* Studies of Participation and Leadership. American Council on Education, Washington, 1955.

28. TABA, HILDA, *With Perspective on Human Relations:* A Study of Peer Group Dynamics in an Eighth Grade. American Council on Education, Washington, 1955.

29. WEDGE, BRYANT M., EDITOR, *College Men:* Psycho-Social Studies. Yale University Press, New Haven, Conn. (In press)

30. WITTY, PAUL, EDITOR, *The Gifted Child.* Heath and Co., Boston, 1951.

H. *Functions of Education*

1. ANDERSON, C. ARNOLD, "Regional and Racial Differences in Relations Between Income and Education," *The School Review,* vol. 63, 1955, pp. 38–45.

2. CHAMBERLIN, DEAN, AND ASSOCIATES, *Did They Succeed in College?* Harper and Bros., New York, 1942.

3. COOK, LLOYD ALLEN, AND ELAINE FORSYTH COOK, *Intergroup Education.* McGraw-Hill Book Co., New York, 1954.

4. GLICK, PAUL C., AND HERMAN P. MILLER, "Educational Level and Potential Income," *American Sociological Review,* vol. 21, 1956, pp. 307–312.

5. HAVEMANN, ERNEST, AND PATRICIA SALTER WEST, *They Went to College.* Harcourt, Brace and Co., New York, 1952.

6. HYMAN, HERBERT H., AND PAUL B. SHEATSLEY, "Attitudes Toward Desegregation," *Scientific American,* vol. 195, no. 6, 1956, pp. 35–39.

7. JACOB, PHILLIP E., *Changing Values in College:* An Exploratory Study of the Impact of College Teaching. Harper and Bros., New York, 1957.

8. KNAPP, ROBERT H., AND HUBERT B. GOODRICH, *Origins of American Scientists.* University of Chicago Press, Chicago, 1952.

9. KNAPP, ROBERT H., AND JOSEPH J. GREENBAUM, *The Younger American Scholar:* His Collegiate Origins. University of Chicago Press, Chicago, 1953.

10. MEAD, MARGARET, *The School in American Culture.* Harvard University Press, Cambridge, Mass., 1951.

11. NEWCOMB, THEODORE M., *Personality and Social Change.* Dryden Press, New York, 1957.

12. ROSE, ARNOLD, *Studies in Reduction of Prejudice.* 2d ed. American Council on Race Relations, Chicago, 1948.

13. SANFORD, NEVITT (ISSUE EDITOR), "Personality Development During the College Years," *The Journal of Social Issues,* vol. 12, no. 4, 1956, pp. 1–70.

14. TABA, HILDA, ELIZABETH HALL BRADY, AND JOHN T. ROBINSON, *Intergroup Education in Public Schools.* American Council on Education, Washington, 1952.

15. WOLFLE, DAEL, AND JOSEPH G. SMITH, "The Occupational Value of Education for Superior High-School Graduates," *Journal of Higher Education,* vol. 27, 1956, pp. 201–212.

I. **The Roles of the Sociologist in Education**

1. BROOKOVER, WILBUR B., *A Sociology of Education.* American Book Co., New York, 1955.

2. COREY, STEPHEN M., *Action Research to Improve School Practices.* Bureau of Publications, Teachers College, Columbia University, New York, 1953.

3. HAVIGHURST, ROBERT J., AND BERNICE L. NEUGARTEN, *Society and Education.* Allyn and Bacon, Boston, 1957.

4. HERRINGTON, GEORGE S., "The Status of Educational Sociology Today," *Journal of Educational Sociology,* vol. 21, 1947, pp. 129–139.

5. LANDIS, JUDSON T., "The Sociology Curriculum and Teacher Training," *American Sociological Review,* vol. 12, 1947, pp. 113–116.